Full Circle Ministry presents:

THE CHARACTER OF CHRIST

Bible Study Series

Mary D. McCorvey

ISBN (Paperback): 979-8-9884037-5-3
ISBN (eBook): 979-8-9884037-4-6

Prayer Letter to Children & Youth Leaders

My prayer is that each lesson will bring your children, youth ministry, small group, worship services, or youth leadership council members, greater confidence in their Spiritual identity and development. I pray that while YOU prepare each lesson, God will breathe His Holy Spirit and wisdom into you. And as you read, study, plan, and make adjustments to meet your ministry needs, you will see *His Hand* and hear *His Voice.* I encourage you to move with God. Although it may feel scary, allow Him to lead. The time that you spend with Him is the best preparation you can ever have!

Read His Word with hunger and teach each lesson with an urgent passion that leaves your students on fire for knowing more about living a life that is *righteous and set apart.* I want to encourage you to be transparent with your students, share your story, and let them know what God has done for you! We have the power to overcome the enemy because of the Blood of the Lamb and by the word of our testimonies! If you have been called to teach and work with adolescents, then *you have a testimony!* Your students need to know what Christ has done for you. Boldly pray that His Spirit will guide your heart on what, how and with whom to share.

Love on your students. You may be the only true Bible they are able to read. Don't get discouraged if they do not appear to be listening or engaged as today's generation processes information in very different ways. ☺

Take care of the seed that you have been given to nurture. As you use these resources, thank God in advance for the *Great Harvest of souls*!

In the Name of Jesus I pray,
AMEN

Table Of Contents

What is Full Circle Ministry? vii

Understanding the GenerationZ Lesson Design.................................ix

Online Teacher Tip Resources..xi

The Character of Christ Overview xiii

Bible Study Series

For Ages 3-5 1

For Ages 6-10 31

For Ages 11-14 65

For Ages 15-18 99

What is Full Circle Ministry?

Full Circle Ministry aims to *fortify the spiritual walls of the new generation.*

With a focus on developing scripturally sound Bible study tools for novice and experienced children and youth ministry workers, each lesson will present a solid foundation on the principles of salvation, prayer and obedience to God.

To support the spiritual development of the new generation of Christ followers, youth leaders and volunteers will be provided with structured lessons that lay the foundation for their students to learn and experience Jesus Christ as they grow. Encourage students to talk, laugh, cry and ask questions as you guide them in their faith journey.

Full Circle Ministry Values:

Student engagement

using

Research-based teaching practices

that incorporate

Culturally relevant and age appropriate examples

For the churched AND unchurched Youth

Understanding the
GenerationZ Lesson Design

The *GenerationZ* lesson structure is modeled after the 5E Lesson Model, a structure used in public school classrooms nationwide, primarily in Science, Social Studies and Math classes. Its predominant strength is that it allows students to make meaning of what they are being taught through using concrete representation, interactive activities, student dialogue, and inquiry.

Each *GenerationZ* Bible lesson plan contains the following elements:

Set It Up:	Each lesson will begin with an opener that briefly introduces your students to what they will be taught. Consider this element as a "structured icebreaker" as it provides students with an opportunity to establish a connection about the topic. *Each **Set It Up** activity has been designed to last no more than five minutes.*
Explore It:	The ***Explore It*** activities do just that…they provide you and your students with an opportunity to dive deeper into what has been presented during the *Set it Up* time. This dialogue is prompted through the use of open-ended questions. Based on your students' responses, adjust the level of questioning to establish an active dialogue based on their understanding. *This section should last about five minutes (however, this can be adjusted based on the conversations).*

Teach It:	The ***Teach It*** section is the "meat" of the lesson. Each GenerationZ lesson plan includes creative ways to present God's Word, such as role-playing, object lessons, and technology integration. Since this is where God's Word should be thoroughly explained, Teacher Notes are included. However, you should never neglect to study the Scriptures for yourself for accurate delivery of the message. *This section can last from ten to fifteen minutes (again, based on the conversations that occur).*
Connect It:	The ***Connect It*** section will bring God's Word and your students' lives together. During this time there should be more "student talk" than "teacher talk". Help your students understand how each lesson's principles apply in their everyday lives, and be prepared to clarify their thinking in a kind and patient manner. *The **Connect It** section is designed to last about ten to fifteen minutes.*
Reflect On It:	At the end of any lesson, there should be a time for participants to reflect on what they have experienced. The ***Reflect On It*** segment provides your students a chance to mentally and spiritually digest what they learned through various activities such as writing/journaling and drawing. ***Reflect On It*** should take about five to seven minutes.
Closing Prayer Points:	Every lesson will end with *three* ***Closing Prayer Points***. These Prayer Points capture the underlying guiding principles of the lesson. You may use these points as you pray collectively at the end of your time with students. Encourage them to incorporate these points into their daily prayer times.

In addition, you will find *Teacher Tips* (for face-to-face and online settings) and *Time to Teach* notes embedded in the lessons to support your planning and creativity process. Please keep in mind that these are recommendations and should not take away from your need to personally study, research, and prepare for your groups.

Online Teacher Tip Resources

Embedded in each lesson are **Online Teacher Tips.** These are suggested ideas on how to intentionally incorporate technology to share the Gospel with more students AND involve parents as their children learn the Word of God regardless of the setting. Before teaching any lesson, preparation is vital, and if you are planning to include the **Online Teacher Tips**, then make sure you are comfortable with the tools, their features, and how they will be used during each lesson.

Included in the *Character of Christ* series, you will find the following online applications and websites, their URLs, and a short description of how it may be used *(description has been taken from each tools' website):*

Flipgrid	https://flipgrid.com/	**Flipgrid** is a tool that allows teachers and students to facilitate video discussions. Each grid is like a message board where teachers can pose questions, called "topics," and their students can post their recorded responses that appear in a tiled grid display. To use Flipgrid simply create an account (*it's FREE and all students will need is their cell phone*).
Kahoot!	https://kahoot.com/	**Kahoot**! is a game-based learning platform that makes it easy to create, share and play learning games or do quizzes in minutes. Unleash the fun in classrooms and living rooms! Students can play on either their phones or on their computers. They will need to have the correct Kahoot code to enter the quiz. *And it's FREE!*

JamBoard	https://jamboard.google.com/	**JamBoard** is an interactive tool that allows students to respond to a question or activity using digital tools (their keyboard) in real-time. **JamBoard** is included in Google's *G Suite* tools. Use the link to get a quick tutorial on JamBoard: https://youtu.be/S9m4HCjOkcA
Padlet	https://padlet.com/	**Padlet** is a web app that lets users post "sticky" notes on a digital wall AND is available with practically any Internet-ready device. You must create a Padlet account. You can use **Padlet** for free, but each free account is allowed only a certain amount of Padlets with limited features.
Google Slides	*Part of Google applications*	**Google Slides** is a presentation program included as part of a free, web-based **Google Docs** office suite offered by **Google**.
PowerPoint	*Part of Microsoft Suite Tools*	Microsoft **PowerPoint** is a presentation software that enables users to create slides, which may contain text, graphics, sound, movies, hyperlinks, and other objects.

The Character of Christ Overview

For today's new generation of Kingdom Builders either to begin or further develop their identity in Christ, it is essential to know His Character. What kind of person was He during His time on this earth? What was in His heart? How did He conduct Himself when He was around other people? As mature Believers, we get it! Right? We know the kind of person that Jesus was. But how do you explain what YOU know and make it relatable to your students?

This series will highlight how Jesus thought, served, and interacted with people during His earthly ministry. The scripture, Philippians 2:5-11, provides the Biblical foundation for each lesson. It opens a window for your students to learn about Christ's character while providing them with opportunities to reflect on their own character. There are many factors that can be highlighted from this selected Scripture. The lessons address three major character traits: *Service, Attitude, and Obedience.* Regardless of the age group you teach, these three areas resonate loudly with parents, teachers, church, and community leaders as being areas where adolescents find great conflict. Kids have admitted that they find themselves fighting bad attitudes and thoughts, battling disobedience, and not being concerned about serving/helping/ministering to other people.

So allow this resource to be a *Spiritual gateway* that leads your students' thoughts and minds to Christ. Provide them with the tools they will need to live an obedient life.

Allow them to understand what service in God's Kingdom looks like at home, school, and in their neighborhoods.

At the end of each lesson, you will find a "Resource section" that contains the materials for each lesson activity. In addition, there is a resource for you: the *Teacher Planning and Reflections* page. Before you stand to share God's Word to your students, do not neglect your meditation and reflection time, for each topic.

You are not expected to be perfect. However, know that the most important thing you can do in your preparation and planning is to be honest with God. Where are you in being obedient to God? Are your thoughts and actions like Christ? Is He pleased with your service? Spend time reflecting on your personal experiences with each lesson topic so that you can be ready to receive what He has for YOU. And at the end of each lesson, don't forget to think about any questions or concerns that may have been communicated. Continually pray for your students because they need you, even when you're not standing in front of them.

Be Blessed and have lots of FUN!

Full Circle Ministry presents

The Character of Christ

Bible Study Series
for Ages 3-5

Let this mind be in you which was also in Christ Jesus!
Philippians 2:5

Clean and Clear

Purpose: *Understand what it means to be like Christ.*

Learner Outcome: Use props to learn about the mind and character of Christ.

Key Scripture: Philippians 2:3-5 (emphasis on v. 5)

Key Words: mind, thoughts, character

Materials: One empty container of any size, four servings of bottled water (one dirty and three clean), a small Ziploc bag of dirt that will be used to create the dirty water mixture, Character Flags, and water bottle labels (included in the Resource section), hot glue gun (for teacher use only).

Set It Up and Explore It: *Crystal Clear Thoughts*

Teacher Note: For this lesson, the *Set It Up* and *Exploration* portions will be done simultaneously.

Set the empty container on the table, along with the bottle of dirty water and one of the clean bottled waters. Ask students the following questions:

1. What do you think would happen if I let this bottle of clean water get mixed with dirt? *Pick up the glass of clean water and pour it into the empty container. After students begin to respond, slowly begin to pour the dirty water into the same container. Invite their reactions to this new mixture and allow them to share their observations.*
2. Would you still want to drink that water?
3. Why or why not?
4. What do you think you would need to do to stop your water from becoming dirty?

Online Teacher Tip: As you go through the *Set It Up* activity, interact with your students by asking them questions. If parents are supporting their child remotely, instruct them to unmute their microphones so that the students can ask or answer any questions.

Transition Statement: "Today, as we learn about the mind and character of Jesus Christ, we are going to pretend that water is like our mind. We want to protect our thoughts and minds from getting dirty so that we can have the kind of mind that Jesus Christ had."

Explain It: *Reading My Mind*
Use the bottles of water to teach students about the type of mind that we should have.

Label one of the remaining bottled waters as "A Mind Like Christ " and the other bottle as "Not Like Christ". Ask a volunteer to hold the Ziploc bag of dirt. Pose the questions: *Can you see other people's thoughts? Can you see what's going on in someone else's mind?*

> **Teacher Note:** Ask questions in different ways to ensure that students understand the word *thoughts*. You may explain that thoughts come from our brain. Thoughts are what we think about. Since we cannot see a person's heart or brain, we are not able to see the thoughts that may be in their mind.

> **Online Teacher Tip:** This component of the lesson can be executed as a teacher demonstration. Prior to the lesson, ask parents to provide students with at least one bottled water so they can virtually interact with the lesson as it progresses.

Explain to the class that they are going to pretend that the bottles of water are THEIR thoughts. They are going to learn how to keep their minds like Jesus Christ. Use the Character Flags in the *Resource section* and discuss each. These words can describe a person's *behavior, attitude, or thoughts.* While discussing each flag, ask students if the *behavior, attitude, or thought* would be good or bad. After students make their choice, place the flag next to the appropriately labeled bottle. *For every Character Flag that students identify as "Not Like Christ", the volunteer will scoop dirt from the Ziploc bag and add it to that bottle of water.

Make sure to replace the cap and give it a good shake so that the water can appear visibly dirty. By the end, students should have a visual representation of a "good mind" and a "bad mind".

Time to Teach: Using the "Reading My Mind" water display, ask the class to describe the mind that Jesus Christ had. Read Philippians 2:5 and have students repeat it in unison. Still using the water props, explain that we should have the same mind that Jesus had because we are His disciples. Many times, when we become angry or selfish, we may start to think in ways that are not like Christ. So even though people may not be able to see our thoughts, they can SEE our actions and HEAR our words! Jesus did not SAY bad things, nor did He DO bad things. Why? Because He did not allow bad thoughts to come into His mind. So we have to protect OUR thoughts by staying away from songs, people, attitudes, television shows, and other activities that do not portray the mind of Christ. At the beginning of the lesson, your students were able to see clear bottles of water, but one of them became dirty because there were things that were "Not Like Christ". Give your students the chance to share their thoughts on being Christ-minded and how they can avoid becoming unlike Christ due to their behavior, attitude, and thoughts.

Connect It and Reflect On It: "*Good Thoughts Taste Good Too!*"
Still using the props, ask students to select the water they would want to drink. Obviously, they will choose to drink the clean and clear water, and ask them why (for emphasis, take a sip of the clean, clear water). It is easier to sip from the clean and clear water because there was nothing in it that made it hard to take in. When people are around us, we want to have Christ inside of us so that others who are near us will want to take Him into their hearts just like you wanted to take in the clean and clear water.

Review Philippians 2:3-5 and ask them to list other words that would describe *behaviors, attitudes, or thoughts* that Jesus would have.

Give students a copy of the water bottle label (pre-cut) and allow them to decorate it and include THEIR names. Help them to copy the Philippians 2:5 scripture on their labels *(if students are too young to write, have it printed and cut and help them paste it on their labels)*. Once students are done with decorating their label, help them to place it on their water bottle with the hot glue gun. This clean and clear bottle of water will serve as a reminder of how their minds should be like that of Christ.

Teacher Tip: Instead of using the water bottle templates from the Resource section, purchase blank labels for shipping or what would fit on a water bottle. Do not worry about trying to ensure that it covers the entire circumference of the bottle.

Online Teaching Tips:

- *Encourage your students to work with parents and/or siblings as they create their "Mind like Christ" water bottle label. They can use a strip of paper, colors/markers, and tape to create their labels at home. Ask them to write THEIR names on their labels because this bottle of clean water will be a reminder of the kinds of behavior, attitude and thoughts they want to have. Once it is complete, encourage your families to place their "Mind Like Christ" water bottles next to the bed or specific location where they pray.*
- *Ask them to send pictures of their finished water bottles to be included in church postings/social media platforms.*

Closing Prayer Points:

1. Help me to identify the parts of my character that are not Christ-like.
2. Show me how to display Christ-like behavior with what I say, think and do each day.
3. Help me be honest when my thoughts are impure and know that I am still loved if I am not perfect.

Clean and Clear

Lesson Resources Section

- ❖ *Teacher Planning/ Reflection page*
- ❖ *Water Bottle Labels*
- ❖ *Character Flags*

Clean and Clear: Teacher Planning and Reflections

Before the Lesson:

Journal how the Holy Spirit is leading on this topic: possessing the mind of Christ. How does your attitude display Christ-like characteristics? Consider *your personal spiritual journey* with this topic.

_____

_____

_____

What lesson adjustments are anticipated as you prepare for your students?

_____

_____

_____

What physical preparations need to be made for your space or extra resources that need to be acquired prior to your lesson?

_____

_____

_____

After the Lesson:

What questions or issues arose during the lesson that you need to cover in prayer?

List students and/or concerns:

_____

_____

_____

Ages 3-5

Water Bottle Templates

Character Flags

Spending time with God	*Repeating bad words*
Disobeying my parents	*Learning more about Jesus*
Sharing my toy with someone who may not have one	*Hate*
Praising God	*Being grateful for God's blessing*
Speaking kind words to people	*Fighting my neighbor*
Taking something that does not belong to me	*Telling the truth to my family and teachers*

Serve Like Jesus
Age Group: 3-5 and 6-10

Purpose: *Understand what it means to act like Christ.*

Learner Outcome*:* Practice humility and serving others through a classroom experience. *Teachers will work collaboratively to present this lesson to their students.*

Key Scripture: Philippians 2:3-8 *(emphasis on v 5);* John 13: 13-15

Key Words: humility, humble, service, love, obedience

Materials: Items that would be used for a dinner (a table setting that includes paper plates, napkins, cups and plastic utensils, paper table cloth), table and chairs, serving dishes, and light healthy snacks. Humble Acts of Service Strips, additional images for lesson activities, Serving Others Color pages *(included in Resources section)*

Teacher Note: This lesson should be collaboratively taught with both age groups (3-5 and 6-10). The older students will be given the opportunity to serve their younger peers. However, do not tell either group what they will be doing until it is time to begin the class.

When the first activity's plans are announced, silently take note of the change in demeanor of the older students once they learn they will be serving the younger children. Before the students arrive, teachers should have the class set up like a dining area (with tables, chairs, and eating utensils). Also, choose the items that will be served. Teachers should be ready to assist in "serving" students as well. If possible, try to have light, healthy snacks ready to serve in order to make the lesson as engaging as possible.

Online Teacher Tip:

1. *Have pictures of a formal table setting ready to share with students on your screen. If parents are participating in the lesson with their students, invite them to set their tables at home prior to the lesson. At the end, ask them to send pictures of their Set It Up experience for church posts.*

Set It Up: "I'm Here to Serve You"

Have the younger students sit in the "dining area" and explain that they are going to be served something to eat as they are learning. Get your older students ready to serve by assigning various tasks (servers, cleaners, food helpers). During this experience, have dialogue with the students about what they are doing.

Encourage the "wait staff" to be kind and courteous as they serve.

Teacher Note: Since this portion of the lesson may take more time than previous *Set It Up* activities, begin posing the "Explore It" questions while students are still partaking in their "meal".

Explore It: "Here to Serve Explored"

Pose the following questions to students even though they may be eating or serving:

1. How many of you have gone out to eat with your parents or other family members? Who came to take your order or bring you water?
2. **For the older students:** Do you think it is always easy to serve people? Why or why not?
3. **For the younger students:** Do you think Jesus would serve people the way you were served today?
4. **For the older students:** Do you think Jesus would serve people the way you served today?

Transition Statement: "In this lesson, we are going to find out why it is important to have the same thoughts and behavior that Jesus had."

Explain It: "The Greatest is the Least"

Show students the following YouTube video: The Greatest is the Least *(click the link).*

This is an animation that shows the story of Jesus washing His disciples' feet. Before showing the video, make sure that students are prepared to recognize the following:

1. *Who Jesus is*
2. *What Jesus is doing in the video*
3. *How Jesus is doing what He is doing*

Teacher Note: Read John 13:13-15. Talk to students about why this was important in the life of the disciples *(emphasis on verse15)*. Jesus wanted to give His disciples an example, and since we are Christians and disciples of Christ, we follow the same example.

If necessary, allow students to watch the video as many times as needed to ensure they see the important things that are occurring. During the first viewing simply allow students to observe without questions. However, during the second viewing, ask and answer any questions students may have and encourage discussion.

Online Teacher Tips:

1. *During the lesson, teachers can share their screens and watch the YouTube video during the lesson. To save time, make sure that the video is ready to go (minimized) and that screen can be shared.*

Time to Teach: After viewing the video, focus on the questions from the Explain It section, particularly questions 2 and 3. Remind students that Jesus was God's Son and He chose the disciples to follow Him. So it would seem like the disciples should have washed Jesus's feet. Right? Give an example: *Would you expect a king or queen of a country to wash a homeless person's feet?* Jesus washed His disciples' feet to show them how to be humble and show love to others. Read Philippians 2:3-8 with the students and discuss what this means. Get your students to talk about the kind of attitude they think Christ had. How would WE know the kind of attitude Jesus had since we were not there to experience it? Make a connection between how Jesus treated His disciples and the example He set through His actions. Teach students the definition of <u>humble</u> and have them repeat it in unison: **Humble** *means being gentle, peaceful, and obedient.* While Jesus was washing His disciples' feet, He did not think that it was disgusting or not cool. Instead, His attitude and actions were *gentle, peaceful, and obedient*. Remind your students that their act of service does not have to be something large and extravagant *(which is the purpose of the "Thumbs Up for Humble Acts" activity)*. It's not about the size of the act or the number of people who know about it. Serving others is about demonstrating the mind of Christ.

Connect It: "Thumbs Up for Humble Acts"

This portion of the lesson will be another interaction between both groups of students. Distribute at least one *Humble Acts of Service* strip to the older students. Explain that they will need to demonstrate the humble act of service on the strip they received. However, their act of service is to be directed to a younger student, forming a partnership. As the act is being done, each new partnership should discuss if they have received an act of humility. If they think their act showed humility *(peacefulness, gentleness and obedience)*, then put a thumbs up. If their act was not humble, then put a thumbs down.

Online Teacher Tips:

1. *Use pictures from the internet (current events) that can be shown on-screen. Students can do "Thumbs Up/Thumbs Down" action to determine if what they see would be an act of humility (being gentle, peaceful and obedient).*
2. *If an online chat is available, students can type an act of humility they have either demonstrated or have seen being demonstrated in the chat box.*

Reflect On It: To close the lesson, divide students into mixed-age groups depending upon the number of students you have *(but no more than five)*. Give each group a piece of chart paper and markers. Allow them to work together to create an image of how they can demonstrate Christ's character. Give them examples and reminders from the lesson. Allow each group about 7-10 minutes to work. At the end of the time, give each group a chance to share their poster with the other groups.

Teacher Note: Create a small circle group for students who may be too young to participate in this *Reflect On It* activity. Discuss the color pages at the end of the *Resources* section. Allow students to fill in the blank with their thoughts about what is taking place in the picture and connect it to how it shows the character of Christ through serving others. Give them time to color the picture that they choose.

Closing Prayer Points:

1. Help me to know more about Jesus.
2. Help me to be gentle, peaceful, and obedient towards other people.
3. Help me to always seek to serve and love others like Jesus did.

Serve Like Jesus

Lesson Resources Section

- ❖ *Teacher Planning/ Reflection page*
- ❖ *Humble Acts of Service Strips*
- ❖ *Additional images for lesson activities (4)*
- ❖ *Serving Others Color pages (3)*
- ❖ *The Greatest is the Least YouTube link:*

  https://www.youtube.com/watch?v=fmtAMUuFfkk&feature=y outu.be

Serve Like Jesus: Teacher Planning and Reflections

<u>Before the Lesson:</u>

Journal how the Holy Spirit is leading you on this topic; ***Service/Serving Others***.

Consider *your personal spiritual journey* with this topic.

_____

_____

_____

What lesson adjustments are anticipated as you prepare for your students?

_____

_____

_____

What physical preparations need to be made for your space or extra resources that need to be acquired prior to your lesson?

_____

_____

_____

<u>After the Lesson:</u>

What questions or issues arose during the lesson that you need to cover with prayer?

List students and/or concerns:

_____

_____

_____

Humble Acts of Service strips

Humble Act of Service:
Find someone whose shoelace is untied and offer to tie it for them.

Humble Act of Service:
Find someone who may need a hug or a handshake.

Humble Act of Service:
Find someone who needs help cleaning up his/her area.

Humble Act of Service:
Find someone who needs help with an assignment.

Humble Act of Service:
Find someone who needs to know that God loves him/her.

Humble Act of Service:
Find someone who needs help fixing his/her clothing.

Humble Act of Service:
Find someone who may need someone to talk to.

Humble Act of Service:
Find something to share with someone else.

Humble Act of Service:
Find someone and pray for them.

Images that can be used for the lesson

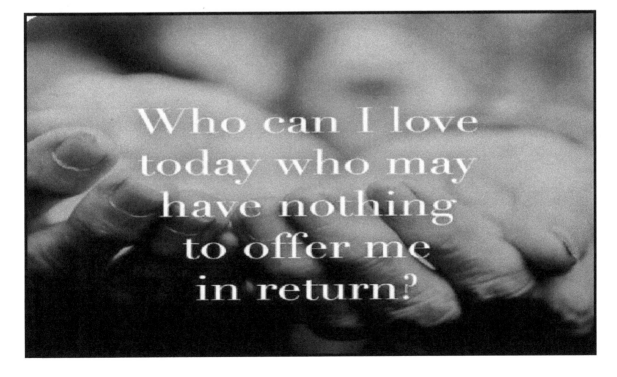

Serving Others color pages

I can show love to others by_____.

I can show love to others by _____.

Serving Others color pages

I can show love to others by_____.

I can show love to others by _____.

I can serve and show love to others by_____.

What is Obedience?

Purpose: *Understand the importance of obedience.*

Learner Outcome: Make choices about being obedient to God and parents.

Key Scriptures: Ephesians 6:1-3; Luke 2:49

Key Words: obedience, disobedience

Materials: YouTube access; colors and other art supplies; tape or glue; Construction or tag paper; *Choose* activity cards *(included in Resource section)*

Set It Up: "The Meaning of Obedience-Explored"
Ask students the following questions:

1. *What does obedient mean? Do you have an example of obedience you would like to share?*
2. *What does disobedient mean?*
3. *Do you think it is better to be obedient or disobedient? Why?*
4. *What do you think God wants us to be; Obedient or Disobedient?*

Teacher Note: During this lesson, try to demonstrate the difference between the words *obedient and disobedient* as much as possible. Because your students are so young, they need concrete and visible examples. Using these words in contrast will provide them with a solid understanding and not leave it as an abstract concept in their minds. Use the contrast in a "back-to-back" manner so that the meaning of one word immediately follows the meaning of the other *(this is modeled in the lesson)*.

Transition Statement: *"Today we are going to learn what the words obedient and disobedient mean and why being obedient is so important to God"*

Teacher Note: The selected YouTube video for the lesson is rather lengthy, so it will be divided in two segments. After each segment, there are questions so that you can monitor your students' understanding.

Explore It: "Tuffy's Tangle with Disobedience"
Students will watch the YouTube video <u>Character Builders-Episode 11-Obedience</u>

Tuffy, who used to be "bad", is learning to have better behavior. When Tuffy goes on a field trip with his teacher and classmates, he learns an important lesson about obedience and disobedience. Stop video at 5:00

Teach It: "The Trouble With Tuffy"
After Part 1 has ended, ask students the following questions:

1. *What was Tuffy excited about?*
2. *What did Tuffy's teacher tell him and his class to do?*
3. *What did Tuffy do instead?*
4. *What was the difference between what Tuffy and Stevie did?*

Stop video at 8:25 and ask students the following questions:

1. *What ended up happening to Tuffy?*
2. *Do you think this happened because Tuffy was obedient or disobedient?*

At the end, ask the following question:

1. *Do you think God likes it when you disobey Him? What about when you disobey your parents or teachers?*

Time to Teach: Define obedience: *Obedience is being free to follow those placed over you.* Obedience is doing what God wants us to do. So when we are disobedient, we are NOT doing what God wants us to do. God expects us to be obedient to Him AND to our parents.

Read Ephesians 6: 1-2. Focus on verse 1, and ask the following question:

- What does Paul say is right? *Obeying our parents.*

So when we are obedient, we make God happy! If we want to be like Christ, then we must obey God and our parents. Why? *Because this is what Jesus did!* He obeyed God, His Heavenly Father, and He also obeyed Mary and Joseph, who were His parents on earth. Read and explain the following scriptures:

- Luke 2: 49-*Jesus obeyed God*
- Ephesians 6: 2-3 *the rewards of being obedient*

Now let's talk about disobedience. If being obedient makes God happy, then what happens when we are disobedient? Refer to the moments in the cartoons when Tuffy was disobedient:

- *Who was Tuffy disobedient to?*
- *How did Tuffy feel when he was being disobedient?*

Talk about what could happen when we are disobedient to God, to parents, and even to teachers.

Connect It: "God Says/What Would Jesus Do?"
This game will be modeled after the playground favorite, *Simon Says.* Instead of following frivolous commands, give your students Godly commands, such as *"God says love your enemies".* They will determine if they will move forward based on whether what you tell them to do would show obedience to God. At the end of each command, allow students to communicate why they moved forward. What would Jesus do if He was given the command?

Teacher Tip: If time permits, allow students to think of other Godly commands to give their peers. Remember that the purpose of the *Connect It* activities from each lesson will allow your students to make decisions about how what they learn will relate to their lives. Allowing them to identify examples of Godly commands will help them make connections with what obedience should look like in their own lives.

Online Teacher Tip: This activity can be done virtually as well. Invite students have their cameras on (with parental support) so that their motions are visible. Even in online settings, physical movement is critical for engagement.

Reflect On It: "I Choose"

Prior to beginning your class, cut the construction or tag paper in half and let students write their names on one half to create a *Name Card (decorating is optional)*. Have the *I Choose* strips cut and spread out. Explain to students that they are going to choose something to work on that will help their minds and character be more like Jesus Christ. Just as we can choose to be disobedient, we can also choose to be obedient. Talk with your kids as they select their *I Choose* strip. Once they have selected their strip, ask them to tell a peer why they chose it (and vice versa). They can tape or glue their strip to their name card. Communicate with parents what their child selected for obedience accountability in the week ahead.

Teacher Tip: Although this activity is similar to the previous *Connect It* activity, the difference is that your students will decide on what they will work on this week. Remind them that disobeying God is not a good thing. But if we have been disobedient, God will forgive us and allow us another chance to be obedient. Be prepared to support your students as they choose what they will work on. Explain that God notices obedience and disobedience to parents and teachers as well. Remind them that Christ was obedient to God AND to Mary and Joseph. His earthly parents. So if they want to have the character of Christ, then obedience is important.

Online Teacher Tip: If parents are participating with their children, consider creating PowerPoint slides that list the "*I Choose*" statements from the Resource section. This will allow your students and parents to see and discuss them. Encourage your students to identify what they will choose to work on so that they can become more obedient to God. Also allow students to add them in your online Chat Box so that they can be shared with others. Continue to emphasize obedience to God.

Closing Prayer Points:

1. *Lord, help me remember that I must be obedient to God because I am Your child.*
2. *Help me be obedient to my parents, teachers, coaches and other adults in authority.*
3. *Because I love God, help me respond with a good attitude when I am expected to be obedient.*

What is Obedience?

Lesson Resources Section

- ❖ *Teacher Planning/ Reflection page*
- ❖ *I Choose Activity Strips*
- ❖ *Tuffy's Tangle with Disobedience YouTube link:*

    https://www.youtube.com/watch?v=2Jz4ZpCgnXI&feature=youtu.be

What Is Obedience: Teacher Planning and Reflections

<u>Before the Lesson:</u>

Journal how the Holy Spirit is leading you on this topic of **Obedience**. Consider *your personal spiritual journey* with this topic.

_____

_____

_____

What lesson adjustments are anticipated as you prepare for your students?

_____

_____

_____

What physical preparations need to be made for your space or extra resources that need to be acquired prior to your lesson?

_____

_____

_____

<u>After the Lesson:</u>

What questions or issues arose during the lesson that you need to cover with prayer?

List students and/or concerns:

_____

_____

_____

I Choose to obey God by praying.

I Choose to obey God by loving people who may not love me.

I Choose to obey God by sharing with other people.

I Choose to obey God by telling other people about Him.

I Choose to obey God by doing what God says to do.

I Choose to obey God by obeying my parents every day.

I Choose to obey God by telling the truth.

I Choose to obey God by being kind to people who are not kind to me.

I Choose to obey God by praying.

I Choose to obey God by doing what God tells me to do.

I Choose to obey God by sharing with others.

I Choose to obey God by obeying my parents every day.

Full Circle Ministry presents

The Character of Christ

*Bible Study Series
for Ages 6-10*

*Let this mind be in you which was also in Christ Jesus!
Philippians 2:5*

Online Teacher Tip Resources

Embedded in each lesson are **Online Teacher Tips.** These are suggested ideas on how to incorporate technology to teach the lessons. By incorporating these resources, as a Youth Pastor, Teacher or Volunteer, you have the chance to share the Gospel with more students AND involve parents as their children take part in learning the Word of God remotely. Before teaching any lesson, preparation is vital, and if you are planning to include the **Online Teacher Tips**, then make sure you are comfortable with the tools, their features and how they will be used during each lesson.

Included in the *Character of Christ* series, you will find the following online applications and/or websites, their URLs and a short description of how it may be used *(description has been taken from each tools' website):*

Flipgrid	https://flipgrid.com/	**Flipgrid** is a tool that allows teachers and students to facilitate video discussions. Each grid is like a message board where teachers can pose questions, called "topics," and their students can post their recorded responses that appear in a tiled grid display. To use Flipgrid, simply create an account *(it's FREE and all students will need is their cell phone).*
Kahoot!	https://kahoot.com/	**Kahoot**! is a game-based learning platform that makes it easy to create, share and play learning games or do quizzes in minutes. Unleash the fun in classrooms and living rooms! Students can play on either their phones or on their computers. They will need to have the correct Kahoot code to enter the quiz. *And it's FREE!*
JamBoard	https://jamboard.google.com/	**JamBoard** is an interactive tool that allows students to respond to a question or activity using digital tools (their keyboard) in real time. **JamBoard** is included in Google's *G Suite* tools. Use the link to get a quick tutorial on JamBoard: https://youtu.be/S9m4HCjOkcA

Padlet	https://padlet.com/	**Padlet** is a web app that lets users post "sticky" notes on a digital wall AND be available with practically any Internet-ready device. You must create a Padlet account. You can use Padlet for free, but each free account is allowed only a certain amount of Padlets with limited features.
Google Slides	*Part of Google applications*	**Google Slides** is a presentation program included as part of a free, web-based **Google Docs** office suite offered by **Google**.
PowerPoint	*Part of Microsoft Suite Tools*	Microsoft **PowerPoint** is a presentation software that enables users to create slides, which may contain text, graphics, sound, movies, hyperlinks, and other objects.

The Mind of Christ

Purpose: *Understand what it means to be like Christ.*

Learner Outcome: Distinguish between Godly and ungodly behaviors.

Key Scripture: Philippians 2: 1-9

Key Words: character, attitude, humble, humility

Materials: Two medium-sized mirrors that can be displayed (for the skit and *Connect It* activity); Character Flag, Mind Title cards and Philppians 2 scripture handouts (included in the Resource section); highlighters, handheld mirrors; index cards or Post-It Notes

Set It Up: "Mirror, Mirror on the Wall" skit

Teacher Note: Prior to the lesson, find three students, preferably high school to act out the skit for this lesson. Give them time to rehearse prior to the lesson, and encourage your actors to be as authentic as possible. If a live presentation can't be done, then consider recording the skit so that it can be shown to your class.

The purpose of this skit is to demonstrate the difference between behaviors that are humble and those that are not so humble. By the way, this may be a good time to define the word <u>humble</u> to your students as well.

Online Teacher Tip: Pre-record the skit using your older student volunteers. To make a better connection, consider asking some of your students' siblings to participate in the video.

Quick note: If you are using personal technology (cell phone, Ipad), make sure that there is good sound quality since it will be shown across your online conferencing platform.

Explore It: "Mirror, Mirror on the Wall" Explored
Use the following questions to prompt discussion about the *Mirror, Mirror skit*:

1. *What kind of attitude was Felicia showing? How would you know what kind of thoughts she may have had based on what you heard her saying?*
2. *What about Kayla? How would you know what kind of thoughts or attitude she had based on what you heard her saying?*
3. *Based on what you know about Jesus Christ's words and actions, what kind of thoughts or attitude do you think HE had? How do you know?*

Give your students the chance to share any evidence that they may have about Jesus' actions that would help them to identify the kind of attitude He had.

4. *Which one of these girls (Felicia or Kayla) displayed an attitude that was more like Christ? Why?*

Transition Statement: "In today's lesson, we are going to learn more about the mind of Christ and about being humble."

Teach It: "Mind Game"
Prior to the lesson, cut the *Character Flag* strips. Each flag contains a word that is either a characteristic of the mind of Christ or the opposite. However, do not share this with your students. As a whole group, give your students time to sort the words into two distinct categories based on similarities and differences. After this has been done, ask the students to create a name for each group they created.

Teacher Tip: This type of activity is called an *Open Card Sort*. Open card sorting allows students to develop their own understanding of the topic through exploration and inquiry. Provide clear instructions on what they will be doing and allow them time to talk about the *Character Flags* as they do the sort as a group.

Time to Teach: After students have sorted through the flags and created two groups, explain that these words can be used to describe characteristics of a person's personality (*the way a person thinks and acts*). So what does that mean? It means that some people may have good thoughts, and others may have negative ones. Some people may demonstrate nice and loving behaviors, while others may act negative and rude. Think about the girls in the skit, Felicia and Kayla. What kind of characteristics were they displaying? Ask for evidence. Tell your students that the words they just sorted will help them to learn more about the way Jesus thought and acted towards others.

Connect It: "Find the Words"
Distribute the Philippians 2 scripture handout to your students. Divide class into groups no larger than four. As they work together in their groups, help your students look for any words from the verses that were also a part of their Character Flags. Then they will highlight or underline any words that they find.

Teacher Note: Because you may have students from different grade levels and with varying learning styles and needs, be prepared to offer reading assistance. You can choose to either read the passages to your students or choose a student volunteer. For students with Bible apps, support them with reading from the same translation as the Scripture handout for consistency with the word meaning.

Online Teacher Tip: Read the Scripture out loud to your students. Using your platform tools, share Philippians 2: 1-9 verses on your screen. As a suggestion, use Bible Gateway. If you have highlighting tools, then use them to highlight the words from the scripture that correspond with the Character Flags. In addition, invite your students to type any words in the chat box that they think should be highlighted from the verses.

Before moving on to *Reflect On It*, revisit the opening skit and discuss the two main characters, Felicia and Kayla. Talk about their conversations and the characteristics of Christ and humility that have just been discussed. Now ask them to match the Character Flags to one of the mirrors that represented Kayla and Felicia's behavior.

Reflect On It: "The Mirror Is On Me"
Your students will now turn the mirror on themselves by moving to the mirror that reflects THEIR current mindset and characteristics.

- Do they look more like Felicia—*the student who displayed the "it's all about me" attitude*?

  or

- Do they look more like Kayla—*the student who showed more interest in helping others learn about Christ and did not want anything in return*?

Encourage your students to be honest and select the mirror that reflects them. Give each one a handheld mirror and an index card (or *Post-It*) and pen. Allow time for your students to think about what area of their personality needs to resemble Christ more and write it down.

Review the Scripture Slips *(included in the Resource Section)* and let them select the verse that will help them with the concern that they wrote down. Challenge them to learn and repeat it over the next few days. Encourage parents to work with their kids to learn the scripture (and others) that will help them to look more like Christ.

Online Teacher Tip: Prior to the lesson, and without your students' knowledge, ask their parents or guardians to submit an electronic picture of their child to you. Once all the pictures have been collected, create a slideshow that captures each student's face. As the slideshow is being shared, talk about Philippians 2:5 and the lessons they learned from today. Even though people will see our faces when they first meet us, they will also remember if we reflected behavior that is Christ-like! Still give them the opportunity to think about something that does not resemble the mind of Christ and have your students write it down. If they are comfortable typing it in the chat box, encourage them to do so, or they can share it with their parents.

Then allow them time to choose a scripture that addresses their spiritual need so that they can learn it at home with their family's support.

Closing Prayer Points:

1. *Help me to identify the parts of my character that are not Christ-like.*
2. *Show me how to display Christ-like behavior with what I say, think and do each day.*

The Mind of Christ

Lesson Resource Section

- ❖ *Teacher Reflection page*
- ❖ *Mirror, Mirror On The Wall skit Philippians 2 Scripture*
- ❖ *Character Flags*
- ❖ *Reflect On It Scripture Slips*

The Mind of Christ: Teacher Planning and Reflections

Before the Lesson:

Journal how the Holy Spirit is leading you on this topic; **possessing the mind of Christ**. How does your attitude display Christ's characteristics? Consider *your personal spiritual journey* with this topic.

_____

_____

_____

What lesson adjustments are anticipated as you prepare for your students?

_____

_____

_____

What physical preparations need to be made for your space or extra resources that need to be acquired prior to your lesson?

_____

_____

_____

After the Lesson:

What questions or issues arose during the lesson that you need to cover with prayer?

List students and/or concerns:

_____

_____

_____

Mirror, Mirror On the Wall

Cast	**3 Students:** **Felicia**: *Otherwise known as the "Mean Girl", Felicia is very stylish, popular, and KNOWS IT!* **Kayla**: *Although Kayla is also popular and athletic, she is extremely humble and kind to others. She goes out of her way to help and show kindness to others.* **Eddie**: *Eddie recently moved to Felicia and Kayla's neighborhood.*
Plot	The two girls are having a conversation in front of their mirrors as they prepare to head to class. The new guy, Eddie approaches them and becomes involved in a conversation about what it means to be humble. Through the students' dialogue, it will become easy to see which mirror displays a humble person and which mirror does not.
Props	Two medium-sized mirrors (Note-Hand mirrors may not be big enough). If you plan to pre-record the skit, have equipment ready and make sure good lighting is available.

Scene: *Both girls are standing in front of their mirror trying to get their look together before heading to a small group Bible study session. Felicia is being "over-dramatic" in front of her mirror while Kayla is simply making sure that her clothes and hair are smooth. She is trying to hurry Felicia along so they won't be late.*

Kayla: Felicia, come on! We've got to get going. I'm not going to let you make us late to the Bible study group! I am looking forward to helping out with the kiddos today and they're depending on our help.

Felicia: Girl, please don't rush me! You KNOW I have to make sure I look good wherever I go! My clothes, makeup and hair MUST be right! You never know who may want to meet ME. And why do we have to go to play with these little kids anyway (with attitude)? We could find so many other things to do...ooh, like the "Don't Rush" Challenge, since you want to rush me!

After both girls laugh, Felicia turns back to her mirror.

Those kids aren't going to care about what we're trying to teach them anyway (rolls eyes). Besides, I was voted "Ms. Popularity" and "Best Dressed" for our high school class. What if one of the kids spills something on ME?

Kayla: Oh my goodness, Felicia! How could ANYONE forget! You're always reminding people, is it all that matters to you? Don't you care about teaching these children about the true meaning of humility? Humility is an incredibly powerful "life lesson"! And it's a characteristic that God expects us to have. So let's start practicing a little humility right now by looking in the mirror!

Both girls start to chuckle and turn from the mirrors. At that time, they notice Eddie, their new neighbor walking towards them.

Felicia (to Kayla): Hey, there's Eddie! You know he's kinda cute, right? I wonder if I can get him to like me. It should be pretty easy...I mean look at me!

(Felicia begins to wave to Eddie and invites him to join them).

What's up, Eddie! Have you started getting used to the new neighborhood yet?

Eddie: Oh, hey ladies! How's it going! Yep, things are going great now that I'm starting to meet more people. Everyone has been really nice.

Kayla: Hey, that's great! You know, Felicia and I are going down to the church to help teach our children's group. Do you want to join us?

Eddie: Help teach the children's group? That sounds interesting! What are you going to be teaching?

Kayla: The lesson is on what it means to be humble. You know, Jesus Christ was so humble, even though He was the Son of God! He still placed other people's needs before Himself. This humility came from His heart. Jesus came to earth to serve others. And because He was He did not BRAG about Himself. His words matched His actions, and His actions showed what was in His heart. And that's how we're supposed to be, too. We just want the kiddos to know why this is so important.

Felicia (showing frustration): How long is this going to take? Kayla, I've already told you that there are other things I could do with my time. And they do NOT include talking all day to little kids about HUMILITY! I know I always look fabulous because I wear the best clothes. And after I graduate from high school, I'm going to the BEST college because MY parents have money to send me anywhere I want to go. So all of this discussion on what it means to be humble does not apply to me. Yeah, I help people out from time to time, but when I need something from them, I expect to be paid back!

Eddie and Kayla look at each other and shake their heads.

Eddie *(to Kayla)*: Um, Kayla, I totally get what you're saying about being humble, and I know Jesus wants us to love others and not to think so highly of ourselves *(glances at Felicia)*. So I'm excited to hear that the children will receive this message. I would love to join you! And Felicia, are you sure you're ready to help with THIS lesson? I'm just saying…*(shrugs shoulders)*.

Felicia: Whatever dude!

Kayla: I just want the students to know about the mind of Christ, and I really want them to know what HUMILITY really looks like.

At this point, Felicia and Kayla turn back to the mirrors they were looking at and stand still while Eddie turns to the students and begins to speak.

Eddie: So what do you guys think? You've heard what both Kayla and Felicia had to say. Pretty interesting, right? But let's think about the last statement that Kayla made. She really wants you guys to know about the mind of Jesus Christ, and what Humility looks like…So let's begin the lesson!

Teacher Tip: Be flexible with the names and genders of students in the script; however, preserve the content. You want your students to have a good understanding of the idea of humility *(since this term seems to be abstract in nature and can be difficult to define to younger students)*. They may recognize the meaning of humility by seeing it be represented before they fully grasp the definition of it.

<u>*Philippians 2: 1-11*</u> *(New Century Version)*

<u>*Verses 1-6*</u>

1) Does your life in Christ give you strength? Does his love comfort you? Do we share together in the Spirit? Do you have mercy and kindness? **2)** If so, make me very happy by having the same thoughts, sharing the same love, and having one mind and purpose. **3)** When you do things, do not let selfishness or pride be your guide. Be humble and give more honor to others than to yourselves. **4)** Do not be interested only in your own life, but be interested in the lives of others. **5)** In your lives, you must think and act like Jesus Christ. **6)** Christ himself was like God in everything. He was equal with God but He did not think that being equal with God was something to boast about.

<u>*Verses 7-11*</u>

7) He gave up his place with God and made himself nothing. He was born to be a man and became like a servant. **8)** And when he was living as a man, he humbled himself and was fully obedient to God. He obeyed even when that caused his death—death on a cross. **9)** So God raised Christ to the highest place. God made the name of Christ greater than every other name. **10)** God wants every knee to bow to Jesus—everyone in Heaven, on earth, and under the earth. **11)** Everyone will say "Jesus Christ is Lord" and bring glory to God the Father!"

Servant	**Compassionate**
Inconsiderate	**Selfish**
Peacebreaker	**Unkind**
Patient	**Dishonest**

Unforgiving	**Obedient**
Generous	**Encouraging**
Conceited	**Gentle**
Bullyish	**Loving**

Reflect On It Scripture Slips

Save me, Lord, from lying lips and from deceitful tongues. **Psalm 120:2**
The Lord detests lying lips, but He delights in people who are trustworthy. **Proverbs 12:22**
For, whoever would love life and see good days must keep their tongue from evil and their lips from deceitful speech. They must turn from evil and do good; they must seek peace and pursue it. **1 Peter 3: 10-11**
If we confess our sins, he is faithful and just to forgive us our sins and to cleanse us from all unrighteousness. **1 John 1:9**
But love your enemies, do good to them, and lend to them without expecting to get anything back. Then your reward will be great, and you will be children of the Most High, because he is kind to the ungrateful and wicked. Be merciful, just as your Father is merciful. **Luke 6:35-36**
Get rid of all bitterness, rage and anger, brawling and slander, along with every form of malice. Be kind to one another, tenderhearted, forgiving one another, as God in Christ forgave you. **Ephesians 4:31-32**
A new commandment I give to you, that you love one another: just as I have loved you, you also are to love one another. By this all people will know that you are my disciples, if you have love for one another. **John 13: 34-35**
Thou shall not steal. **Exodus 20:15**
So now I am giving you a new commandment: Love each other. Just as I have loved you, you should love each other. **John 13:34**
Most important of all, continue to show deep love for each other, for love covers a multitude of sins. **1 Peter 4:8**

Serve Like Jesus

*Age Group: 3-5 and 6-10

Purpose: *Understand what it means to act like Christ.*

Learner Outcome: Practice humility and serving others through a classroom experience.

Teachers will work collaboratively to present this lesson to their students.

Key Scripture: Philippians 2: 3-8 *(emphasis on v 5),* John 13: 13-15

Key Words: humility, humble, service, love, obedience

Materials: Items that would be used for a dinner (a table setting that includes paper plates, napkins, cups and plastic utensils, paper table cloth), table and chairs, serving dishes and light healthy snacks. Humble Acts of Service Strips, additional images for lesson activities, Serving Others Color pages *(included in Resources section)*

Teacher Note: In this learning experience, the older students (6-10) will be given the charge to serve their younger peers (3-5). However, do not tell either group what they will be doing until it is time to begin the class. When the first activity's plans are announced, silently take note of the noticeable change in the demeanor of your older students once they learn that they will be serving the younger ones. Before your students arrive, set your class up like a dining area (with table, chairs and eating utensils). Consider having light, healthy snacks ready to serve in order to make the lesson as engaging as possible. Be ready to assist in "serving" your students as well.

Online Teacher Tip: Have pictures of a formal table setting ready to share with students on your screen. If parents are participating in the lesson with their students, invite them to set their tables at home prior to the lesson to participate in the experience as well. At the end, ask them to send pictures of their *Set It Up* experience for any church posts.

Set It Up: "I'm Here to Serve You"
Have the younger students sit in the "dining area" and explain that they are going to be served something to eat as they are learning. Get your older students ready to serve by by assigning various tasks *(servers, cleaners, food helpers)*. During this experience, talk with the students about what they are doing. Encourage the "wait staff" to be nice and courteous as they serve.

Teacher Note: Since this portion of the lesson may take more time than previous *Set It Up* activities, begin asking the *Explore It* questions while students are still partaking in their "meal".

Explore It: "Here to Serve" Explored
After the *Set It Up* activity, pose the following questions to students:

1. *How many of you have gone out to eat with your parents or other family members? Who came to take your order or bring you water?*
2. **For the older students:** *Do you think it is always easy to serve people? Why or why not?*
3. **For the younger students:** *Do you think Jesus would serve people the way you were served?*
4. **For the older students:** *Do you think Jesus would serve people the way you served?*

Transition Statement: "In this lesson, we are going to find out why it is important to have the same thoughts and behavior that Jesus had."

Explain It: "The Greatest is the Least"
Show students the following YouTube video: **The Greatest is the Least** *(click the link)*.

This is an animation that shows the story of Jesus washing His disciples' feet. Before showing the video, make sure that students recognize the following:

1. *Who Jesus is*
2. *What Jesus is doing in the video*
3. *How Jesus is doing what He is doing*

Teacher Note: Read John 13:13-15. Talk to students about why this was important in the life of the Disciples *(emphasis on verse15)*. Jesus wanted to give His disciples an example, and since we are Christians and disciples of Christ, we follow the same example.

If necessary, allow students to watch the video as many times as needed to make sure they see the important aspects that are being communicated. During the first viewing, simply let students observe with no questions. However, during the second viewing, ask and answer any questions students may have.

Online Teacher Tips:

1. *During the lesson, teachers can share their screen and watch the YouTube video during the lesson. To save time, ensure the video is ready to go (minimized) and that screen can be shared.*

Time to Teach: After viewing the video, focus on the questions from the Explain It section, particularly questions 2 and 3. Remind students that Jesus was God's Son and He chose the disciples to follow Him. So it would seem like the disciples should have washed Jesus's feet. Right? Make an example: *Would you expect a king or queen of a country to wash a homeless person's feet?* Jesus washed His disciples' feet to show them how to be humble and show love to others. Read Philippians 2:3-8 with the students and discuss what this means. Get your students to talk about the kind of attitude they think Christ had. How would WE know the kind of attitude Jesus had since we were not there to experience it? Make a connection between how Jesus treated His disciples and the example He set through His actions. Teach students the definition of <u>humble</u> and have them repeat it in unison: ***Humble*** *means being gentle, peaceful and obedient.* While Jesus was washing His disciples' feet, He did not think that it was disgusting or not cool. Instead His attitude and actions were *gentle, peaceful and obedient.* Also remind students that their act of service does not have to be something large and extravagant (which is the purpose of the "Thumbs Up for Humble Acts" activity). It's not about the size of the act or the number of people who know about it. Serving others is about demonstrating the mind of Christ.

Connect It: *"*Thumbs Up for Humble Acts"

Before jumping into the Acts of Service activity, show your students the following video on Sanya Pirani *(transcript is included in Resources section)*

Sanya Pirani interviewed by WCCO Rachel Slavik 3/18/17

This video showcases the work of a young teenager who had a heart for helping others starting at the age of eight! Feel free to give your students the context for this video by sharing some details from Sanya' story (from her website).

This portion of the lesson will be another interaction between both groups of students. Distribute at least one *Humble Acts of Service* strip to the older students. Explain that they will need to demonstrate the humble act of service on the strip they received. However, their act of service is to be directed to a younger student, forming a partnership. As the act is being done, each new partnership should discuss if they have received an act of humility. If they think their act showed humility *(peaceful, gentleness and obedience)*, then put a thumb up. If their act was not humble, then put a thumb down.

Online Teacher Tips:

1. *Use pictures from the internet (current events) that can be shown on-screen. Students can do "Thumbs Up/Thumbs Down" action to determine if what they see would be an act of humility (being gentle, peaceful and obedient).*
2. *If an online chat is available, students can type an act of humility they have either demonstrated or seen being demonstrated in the chat box.*

Reflect On It: To close the lesson, divide students into mixed age groups depending upon the number of students you have *(but no more than five)*. Give each group a piece of chart paper and markers. Allow them to work together to create an image of how they can demonstrate Christ's character. Give them examples and reminders from the lesson.

Allow each group about 7-10 minutes to work. At the end of the time, give each group a chance to share their poster.

Teacher Note: Create a small circle group for students who may be too young to participate in this *Reflect It* activity. Discuss the color pages at the end of the *Resources* section. Allow students to fill in the blank with their thoughts about what is taking place in each picture and connect it to how it shows the character of Christ through serving others. Give them time to color the picture that they choose.

Closing Prayer Points:

1. Help me to know more about Jesus.
2. Help me to be gentle, peaceful and obedient towards other people.
3. Help me to always seek to serve and love others like Jesus did.

Serve Like Jesus

Lesson Resources Section

- ❖ *Teacher Planning/ Reflection page*
- ❖ *Humble Acts of Service Strips*
- ❖ *Additional images for lesson activities (4)*
- ❖ *Sanya Pirani's Story* (transcript from website)
- ❖ Sanya Pirani Interview YouTube link: *https://youtu.be/eV6ZlrBNTAc*
- ❖ *The Greatest is the Least* YouTube link: *https://youtu.be/fmtAMUuFfkk*

Serve Like Jesus: *Teacher Planning and Reflections*

<u>Before the Lesson:</u>

Write down how the Holy Spirit is leading you on this topic: ***Service/Serving Others***.

Consider *your personal spiritual journey* with this topic.

_____

_____

_____

What lesson adjustments are anticipated as you prepare for your students?

_____

_____

_____

What physical preparations need to be made for your space or extra resources that need to be acquired prior to your lesson?

_____

_____

_____

<u>After the Lesson:</u>

What questions or issues arose during the lesson that you need to cover with prayer?

List students and/or concerns:

_____

_____

_____

Humble Acts of Service strips

Humble Act of Service:
Find someone whose shoelace is untied and offer to tie it for them.

Humble Act of Service:
Find someone who may need a hug or a handshake.

Humble Act of Service:
Find someone who needs help cleaning up his/her area.

Humble Act of Service:
Find someone who needs help with an assignment.

Humble Act of Service:
Find someone who needs to know that God loves him/her.

Humble Act of Service:
Find someone who needs help fixing his/her clothing.

Humble Act of Service:
Find someone who may need someone to talk to him/her.

Humble Act of Service:
Find something to share with someone else.

Humble Act of Service:
Find someone and pray for them.

Images that can be used within lesson

THE STORY OF HOW IT STARTED

From a very young age, I used to worry about kids who do not have a mother and father. I used to wonder who feeds them. Who gives them clothes, especially in winter? Who keeps them warm and who reads them stories at night?

One night, I peeked in my mother's office, she was watching a YouTube video clip of children suffering due to war; I saw a girl who looked younger than me sitting on the ground with torn clothes, no shoes, immense sadness and fear in her eyes. I was sad, angry and worried for her. I ran away to my room. Her sad eyes told me "Help me."

Later, my mother had asked me what was bothering me. I told her that I saw that girl who was sitting on the ground on the YouTube video. Was it real? "Why did she look so sad and helpless?" My mother reluctantly explained that the girl perhaps lost her family and might not have anyone to care for her. I immediately asked, "Why? Mother, didn't you tell me God loves everyone?"

My Mother replied, "Of course."

"So why are some people extremely poor and others are not?" I asked.

My Mother replied, "God created people like you and others who are passionate about helping God's children."

That night my mother's words became real to me. I decided I needed to do something big to help others. Now the question in my mind was what should I do that will not only have a big impact but also to inspire my friends to collaborate with me.

The next morning I woke up early and started googling the ways to help. I came across a website that explained how I could feed a village of 100 people for one year.

Boy I was thrilled! I couldn't wait to tell my mother. When I told her my plans she said, "How about starting with feeding one child first?"

I looked at my mother and said, "You told me, I could reach for the star in me." Mother knew at this point that nothing could stop me.

Taken from: *Sanya's Hope for Children* website https://www.sanyashopeforchildren.org/

Obedience is the Key

Purpose: *Understand the importance of obedience.*

Learner Outcome: Make decisions about obedience to God and others.

Key Scriptures: Colossians 3:20 and Ephesians 6:1-3; Joshua 6:1-21; Genesis 22: 1-12; 6:9-22; Philippians 2:6-11

Key Words: obedience, obey, disobedience, disobey

Materials: Prepared Drama box (see Teacher Note below), YouTube access, index cards, construction paper (cut into the size of the postcards), stickers, stencils and other craft supplies that can be used for postcard decorations, markers, Hula Hoop (or something that can be shaped into an "O". You can even use masking tape to make the shape on the floor); Blank postcards to show your students.

Teacher Note: Prior to the lesson, give yourself enough time to gather supplies for your Drama Box. Since the *Teach It* activity will be based on scripture plots, make sure that what is included in the box are items that correspond to the story *(hammer, nails, crown, etc)*. Be creative as you load your boxes. Visit your local dollar and thrift stores AND check your arts and crafts stash and toolbox.

Set It Up: **"Simon Says"**
This lesson will kick off with a rousing round of "Simon Says"! *Explain the game to students if they do not know (or don't remember) how to play this classic childhood game.* Play the game for no longer than three minutes.

Explore It: **"Simon Says-Explored"**
After the game has been played, ask students the following questions:

1. What is the "rule" of *Simon Says*? *(No one can perform a movement until "Simon Says". Doing so results in a penalty.)*
2. So let's pretend that the game, *Simon Says, is* like our life. What lesson do you think this game could teach us? *(How to be obedient; how to follow instructions)*
3. As Chrstians, if this game teaches us how to be obedient, then whose instructions should we be prepared to follow? *(God)*
4. What does God expect from those who follow Him? *(To follow the instructions He gives; To obey Him)*

> **Online Teacher Tip:** 1) Consider asking someone to demonstrate playing this game with you so that students can watch it being played out. 2) Parents, guardians and other family members can play along at home as well. If the second option is selected, you can serve as "Digital Simon", or ask family members to play their own round of the game while you facilitate the online engagement. Make sure to set a timer.

Transition Statement: In this lesson, we are going to learn that if we have a relationship with God, then He expects us to be obedient to Him.

Teach It: "God Said It and That Settles It"
Before beginning the lesson, make sure that your students clearly understand the difference between being *obedient* and *disobedient by giving everyday examples.*

Divide students into four groups of mixed ages and assign one of the following Bible passages to each group:

- *Joshua—Joshua 6: 1-21*
- *Abraham—Genesis 22: 1-12*
- *Jesus—Philippians 2: 6-11*
- *Noah—Genesis 6: 9-22*

> **Teacher Note**: Instead of all four, you may choose to assign only three *(based on the number of students present and amount of time you have)*. However, it is important that one group is assigned to discuss the Philippians 2 passage.

Once the groups have been created, they will take the following steps to while studying their passages: *1) identify what God's instructions were to each person and 2) discuss each Biblical person's response.* Then they will prepare a dramatization of their assigned passage using props from the Drama Box. Each group will showcase their presentation to the other groups.

Importantly, at the end of their presentation, they must include what God said and each Biblical person's response to God's instructions. Encourage your students to be as creative as possible. Allow 15-20 minutes for this portion of the lesson.

Online Teacher Tip:

1. *If you are using an online meeting platform, use the breakout room feature to divide your students into small groups. If you use this feature, enlist the support of other adult volunteers, perhaps a few parents, or older youth to support the small group dialogue.*

2. *If using breakout rooms is <u>not</u> an option, then select one other Bible passage to share (in addition to Philippians 2) to use in your lesson. If you select to present the Biblical passages yourself, then use the Drama Box items as part of your presentation.*

Time to Teach: By the end of each presentation, your students should be able to recognize that each scripture shows obedience to God. Because each person obeyed Him *(Jesus, Noah, Abraham and Joshua)*, freedom followed. *Freedom from death, from condemnation and from being separated from God!* Were any of the tasks that God gave to each person easy and fun to complete? No! God gave each person all of the tools needed to get the task done. However, when we disobey God, there will be no freedom. The more we trust Him, the easier it becomes to obey Him. We can't expect to follow our own rules and get the results of someone else's rules. That doesn't make sense! The more we obey God the more we will see how being obedient produces freedom.

Connect It: "The Next Steps"

Teacher Note: This portion of the lesson will connect being *obedient to God* and to *important human beings*. This may bring up a lot of questions from your students. To welcome honest and trusting communication with students, open with the following questions:

Do you think it is ALWAYS easy to be obedient to God? Why or why not?
Do you think it matters if we are obedient or disobedient to parents? Why or why not?

After discussing the questions, allow students to <u>write</u> about a time they may have been disobedient to a *parent, teacher or an adult in authority* on an index card *(allow two minutes)*. After writing, give them time to share what they wrote with another peer. Show the following YouTube video to your students: <u>Three Reasons to Obey Your Parents</u>. Discuss the video once it has ended.

Time to Teach: Obedience is important in the eyes of The Lord. He also has set the expectation for us to obey parents, teachers, police officers and others who may have set rules or instructions for us to follow. There is no freedom in disobeying those in authority, most importantly parents! Read Colossians 3:20 and Ephesians 6:1-3. The Bible tells us that children are to obey their parents. God promises a long life for those who do. So when we do NOT honor our parents and are disobedient to them, then we are also being disobedient to God. Jesus Christ is the Son of God, yet He still obeyed God, even unto death. So what does this mean for us? The more we read and study the Bible, the more we learn what God wants from us.

Take your hula hoop *(or "O" shaped substitute)* and place it in the middle of the floor. Have a conversation with your students about what they may have written on their index card. Following the example from the YouTube video, have students place them in the most appropriate location (outside of the "O").

Online Teacher Tip: Show the YouTube video to your students, and plan to have the same dialogue with them about the importance of obeying parents and other adults.

Suggestion 1: Use the Hula Hoop (or your "O' shaped substitute) as a visual representation and ask students to type examples of obedience and disobedience in the Chat Box. As they share their examples, add them to the appropriate section of the Hula Hoop using the index cards or Post-It notes.

Suggestion 2: Create a free Padlet account and design an interactive bulletin board so that students can add their responses to it. You will need to share the Padlet link to the Chat Box so that your students can access it.

Reflect On It: "Obedience Postcard"
Give your students a piece of the construction paper and prepare them to create an Obedience Postcard *(show the blank postcard and tell what it is used for)*.

Directions for the Obedience Postcard:

1. *Your students will use arts and craft supplies to create an image/design that represents the word obedience. Since it's their image, encourage them to be creative.*
2. The other side will be a message that they will write to someone sharing the following: 1) what they have learned about obedience and 2) how it applies to their life. For example they can write it to *God, a parent, a teacher or a coach.*

As students complete their Postcards, ask them to add them to the INSIDE of the hula hoop space and discuss why this is relevant.

Consider posting some of your students' Obedience Postcards to your church or children ministry's social media platform.

Closing Prayer Points:

1. *Lord help me to remember to be obedient because I am Your child.*
2. *Help me be obedient to my parents, teachers, coaches and other adults in authority.*
3. *Help me to respond with a good attitude when I am expected to be obedient.*

Obedience is the Key

Lesson Resources Section

- ❖ *Teacher Planning/Reflection Page*
- ❖ *Three Reasons to Obey Your Parents YouTube link:*

  https://youtu.be/ZFOzbvGb3uU

Obedience is the Key: *Teacher Planning and Reflections*

<u>Before the Lesson:</u>

Write how the Holy Spirit is leading you on this topic of **Obedience**. Consider *your personal spiritual journey* with this topic.

_____

_____

_____

What lesson adjustments are anticipated as you prepare for your students?

_____

_____

_____

What physical preparations need to be made for your space or extra resources that need to be acquired prior to your lesson?

_____

_____

_____

<u>After the Lesson:</u>

What questions or issues arose during the lesson that you need to cover with prayer?

List students and/or concerns:

_____

_____

_____

Obedience is the Key

Lesson Resources Section

- ❖ *Teacher Planning/Reflection Page*
- ❖ *Three Reasons to Obey Your Parents YouTube link:*

  https://youtu.be/ZFOzbvGb3uU

Obedience is the Key: Teacher Planning and Reflections

<u>Before the Lesson:</u>

Write how the Holy Spirit is leading you on this topic of **Obedience**. Consider *your personal spiritual journey* with this topic.

_____

_____

_____

What lesson adjustments are anticipated as you prepare for your students?

_____

_____

_____

What physical preparations need to be made for your space or extra resources that need to be acquired prior to your lesson?

_____

_____

_____

<u>After the Lesson:</u>

What questions or issues arose during the lesson that you need to cover with prayer?

List students and/or concerns:

_____

_____

_____

Full Circle Ministry presents

The Character of Christ Series

For Ages 11-14

Let this mind be in you which was also in Christ Jesus!
Philippians 2:5

Online Teacher Tip Resources

Embedded in each lesson are **Online Teacher Tips.** These are suggested ideas on how to embed technology to teach the lessons. By incorporating these resources, as a Youth Pastor, Teacher or Volunteer, you have the chance to share the Gospel with more students AND involve parents as their children take part in learning the Word of God remotely. Before teaching any lesson, preparation is vital, and if you are planning to include the **Online Teacher Tips**, then make sure you are comfortable with the tools, their features and how they will be used during each lesson.

Included in the *Character of Christ* series, you will find the following online applications and/or websites, their URLs and a short description of how it may be used *(description has been taken from each tools' website):*

Flipgrid	https://flipgrid.com/	**Flipgrid** is a tool that allows teachers and students to facilitate video discussions. Each grid is like a message board where teachers can pose questions, called "topics," and their students can post their recorded responses that appear in a tiled grid display. To use Flipgrid, simply create an account *(it's FREE) and all students will need is their cell phone.)*
Kahoot!	https://kahoot.com/	**Kahoot**! is a game-based learning platform that makes it easy to create, share and play learning games or do quizzes in minutes. Unleash the fun in classrooms and living rooms! Students can play on either their phones or on their computer. They will need to have the correct Kahoot code to enter the quiz. *And it's FREE!*
JamBoard	https://jamboard.google.com/	**JamBoard** is an interactive tool that allows students to respond to a question or activity using digital tools (their keyboard) in real time. **JamBoard** is included in Google's *G Suite* tools. Use the link to get a quick tutorial on JamBoard: https://youtu.be/S9m4HCjOkcA

Padlet	https://padlet.com/	**Padlet** is a web app that lets users post "sticky" notes on a digital wall AND be available with practically any Internet-ready device. You must create a Padlet account. You can use Padlet for free, but each free account is allowed only a certain amount of Padlets with limited features.
Google Slides	*Part of Google applications*	**Google Slides** is a presentation program included as part of a free, web-based **Google Docs** office suite offered by **Google**.
PowerPoint	*Part of Microsoft Suite Tools*	Microsoft **PowerPoint** is a presentation software that enables users to create slides, which may contain text, graphics, sound, movies, hyperlinks, and other objects.

The Mind of Christ

Purpose: *Understand what it means to be like Christ.*

Learner Outcome: Distinguish between Godly and ungodly behaviors.

Key Scripture: Philippians 2:1-9

Key Words: character, attitude, humble/humility

Materials: Character Flags, human profile shapes *(both included in the Resources section)*, chart paper *(at least three)*, markers, small trash can

Set It Up: "Word Sort"

Teacher Tip: Make sure that your students know what the words mean that are on the Character Flags. Words like *condemn, spiteful* and *humble* may be difficult for them to define, so be prepared to give descriptions. Prior to the lesson, cut the flags into strips.

Students will use the Character Flags to do a card sort. Each flag contains a word that is either a characteristic or not of Christ. Do not tell your students what the categories are. Give them the chance to discover this as they work together as a group to sort through the cards. Once sorted, let students create titles for each group.

Online Teacher Tip:
- Using the Character Flags, create a *Google Slides* presentation using the words. Give your students the opportunity to discuss the words and decide where they should be placed based on similarities and differences. Make sure your students are unmuted so they can talk with each other.
  - One recommendation that allows digital interactions is Google Jamboard
  - (a Google Chrome free extension). Click on the links to view YouTube tutorials for each of these tools.
  - Create Kahoot! This tool will allow you to create a quiz-like game with students. Use either *Christlike and Not Christlike* or *True/False* as the answer choices to get students to determine each Character Flag.

Explore It: "Word Sort Explained"

After the *Set It Up Word Sort*, ask students the following questions:

1. *How did the groups differ from each other?*
2. *Why did you choose to give each group the title you did?*
3. *The reality is that these words can be used to describe someone's behavior or character. What would you think about a person whose behavior or character looked like the words in each of these groups?*
4. *Which set of cards would you think Jesus Christ's character would look the most like?*

Transition Statement: "The character of Jesus Christ was easily recognized by those who followed Him when He lived on earth. Today we will learn why it is just as important for those of us who are Christians to display the same attitude and behavior."

Teach It: "Profile Identification"

Read Philippians 2:1-9 with your students and discuss how these verses provide crucial information about two types of character: *1) the character of Jesus Christ* and 2) *the EXPECTED character of a Christian (someone who follows Christ).*

What are the differences between the behaviors in these verses?

Divide students into two separate groups and give each group a piece of chart paper and markers. They will work together to create a "personality profile" for the person they will be assigned. Assign the groups as follows:

1. *The profile of Jesus Christ*
2. *The (expected) profile of a person who seeks to follow Jesus Christ*

Teacher Tip: Be prepared to explain what a profile is. Based on the number of students you have, create more than two groups if necessary. Four to five students in each group is an optimal number.

Once in groups, instruct your students to carefully re-read the verses. This time they will identify the character traits that could be assigned to their person. Encourage them to be creative as they create their profile *(For example: Draw a human profile on their chart paper and decorate with the words and/or phrases that would describe the characteristics of their assigned person).* After 8-10 minutes, let each group hang their personality profiles. Then give your students time to review them.

Online Teacher Tip: Create breakout rooms based on your conferencing platform. Use the same directions that were provided for the "Profile Identification" activity.

A few suggestions to substitute for the chart paper are:

- *creating a digital whiteboard (based on the platform you have)*
- *adding a JamBoard link for each group*
- *having one student from each breakout group use paper and markers to create the profile and add information from their group discussions*

Set a timer so that students will know when it's time to wrap up this part of the lesson.

Time to Teach: One of the outcomes of this activity is for students to become more familiar with Jesus Christ as a person. Help them understand the structure and organization of the verses they read:

- *Verses 1-4 provide insight on the character and behavior of followers of Christ*
- *Verses 5-9 focus on the profile of Jesus*

Read v 5 again with students. Throughout your lesson, emphasize this verse as much as possible because it is the "bridge" that identifies the <u>expected</u> attitude of humans and the <u>actual</u> attitude of Christ. As Christ's followers, we should have the same attitude that He displayed.

In verses 5-9 we learn the following:

- *In His divine nature, Jesus is the eternal Son of God, the promised Messiah, and exalted by God.*
- *In his human nature, Jesus was a servant of God who came to minister to people.*

Jesus did not boast about being better than others because of His divine nature. Instead, He continued to honor God in everything He did. Even in His death, Jesus remained obedient and humble! What other words can your students think of to describe Christ's character? Add those terms to the profile charts they created.

Connect It: "The Un-Attitude of Christ"

Prepare your chart paper for a third personality profile—*the "Un-Attitude" of Christ*. Now that your students have discussed the mind and attitude of Christ, give them time in their groups to identify the behaviors and attitudes that are NOT like Christ. Even though these assigned verses do not explicitly state an un-Christlike character, use the following question to prompt their responses:

In verse 5, we are instructed to have the mind of Christ. If this is the case, then what would a mind that is NOT like Christ look like?"

As students work in their groups, remind them that they are thinking of words that would be the opposite of the ones they used to describe their assigned person *(Jesus and a person who follows Jesus)*. They can add their words to their chart paper and then give time for a whole group discussion.

Time to Teach: It is important for students to identify *thoughts, behaviors and attitudes* that are not like Christ. You want your students to be able to recognize the areas in their lives that may not line up with His. Remind them of the importance of remaining humble in every area of their lives (with family, school, spiritual, talents and abilities). Not being humble doesn't resemble Christ, so we must pray to have a humble heart instead of exalting ourselves. Because God is Holy, He expects us to be Holy. So anything that does not represent holiness must be cancelled.

Reflect On It: "Take My..."

Give each student a human profile and let them reflect on *their behavior, attitude, character, and thoughts.* They are required to honestly identify what needs to be addressed as they live as Christians. Being like Christ includes honesty, so encourage them to write down any areas in their lives that do not resemble Christ on their cutout. Once everyone has done this, have them bring their cutout to a trash can or designated container to be thrown away. Before having students toss their cutouts, lead them in prayer about ending any unchristlike behaviors and seeking God for support.

Prior to the lesson, decorate your small trash can with catchy phrases that would highlight eliminating unchristlike behaviors and attitudes. Some suggestions for your trash can names:

"Sin Bin", "Attitude Buster Can" or "Bad Behavior Basket".

Online Teacher Tip: Give the same instructions to write down an area of their lives that does not resemble Christ. Let them turn their cameras off while they do this. However, on the count of three (or whatever you decide to use as your signal), instruct them to turn their cameras back on with their paper in front of their camera. If you can sense they are hesitant, you can assure them that you won't share their personal reflections. If they still aren't comfortable sharing, you can reassure them that you will pray for them regardless of knowing the details. As students begin to share what they may have written down, pray for the concerns they are displaying. Then give them a chance to tear them up and toss them in a trash can at home. If parents are participating, ask them to do the same to support their child and family.

Time to Teach: Consider reading 2 Corinthians 5:17 during this *Reflect It* moment and explain that as Christians, we should not hold on to behaviors and attitudes that do not resemble Christ. When we became Christians, we also became new creatures. So we have to <u>choose</u> to stop participating in negative behaviors and conversations and having thoughts that are unlike Christ. When we throw something in the garbage, we don't go back and get things out of it *(or we shouldn't)*. We throw things away that no longer serve us any purpose. As your students throw their unChrist-like profiles away, they are declaring that the things they wrote down no longer have a place in their lives as disciples.

Closing Prayer Points:

1. *Help me to identify the parts of my character that are not Christ-like.*
2. *Show me how to display Christ-like behavior with what I say, think and do each day.*

The Mind of Christ

Lesson Resource Section

- ❖ *Teacher Reflection page*
- ❖ *Character Flags*
- ❖ *Human Profile Cutout*
  (make as many copies as needed)

The Mind of Christ: *Teacher Planning and Reflections*

<u>Before the Lesson:</u>

Write how the Holy Spirit is leading you on this topic: **possessing the mind of Christ**. How does your attitude display Christ's characteristics? Consider *your personal spiritual journey* with this topic.

_____

_____

_____

What lesson adjustments are anticipated as you prepare for your students?

_____

_____

_____

What physical preparations need to be made for your space or extra resources that need to be acquired prior to your lesson?

_____

_____

_____

<u>After the Lesson:</u>

What questions or issues arose during the lesson that you need to cover with prayer?

List students and/or concerns:

_____

_____

_____

Gossips	**Caring**
Generous	**Insensitive to Others**
Patient	**Unforgiving**
Pride	**Humble**

Helpful	**Offends People**
Honest	**Loving**
Unwilling to Listen	**Anger**
Self Control	**Faith**

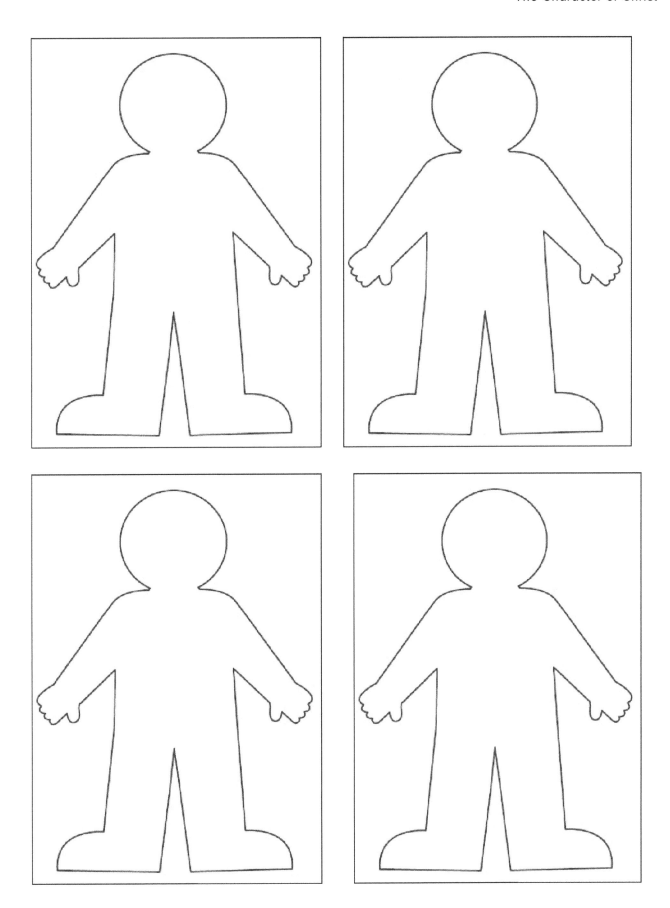

Serving Others

Purpose: *Understand what it means to act like Christ.*

Learner Outcome: Identify the humble acts of Jesus Christ.

Key Scriptures: Matthew 20:28 and 23:11; Matthew 6:1-4; John 13: 1-17 *(for reference)*

Key Words: serve, humble, humility

Materials: blank paper, sample foldable, flip flops for props

---

Set It Up: "Flip Flops"
Show the following video to your students: **Object Lesson on Servanthood – Flip Flops.**

Teacher Tip: If possible, have 1-2 pairs of flip flops on hand to display as props. Students in this age group are able to make better connections when there are concrete representations to go along with what they are learning.

*Prior to the lesson, test your sound to ensure that your settings are properly enabled *(for online preparation)*.

Online Teacher Tip: Share your screen with students using your platform tools. For best results, copy the link address of the video (https://youtu.be/zOU2G2mdtik) and put it in the Chat Box. By doing this, your students will be able to click on the link and watch it on their own devices. This will ensure that there will be no audio or visual interference.

Explore It: "Flip Flops Video Explained"
After students have watched the video, ask the following questions:

1. *Think about what you saw in the video. Do you think it is difficult to help people the way that Jesus did?*
2. *What is something that this video teaches us about the heart, character or behavior of Jesus Christ?*

Time to Teach: Since this lesson will examine *servanthood*, it will be important to establish its meaning with students. Servanthood, or serving others is *sacrificing our time, gifts and resources to help or minister to others who may be in need.* Allow time to briefly share initial thoughts on what it means to make sacrifices to serve others. What does it mean to serve others in today's culture, especially the way Jesus did?

Transition Statement: *"In this lesson, we will learn how to serve others in the same way that Christ did and understand why serving others is so important."*

Teach It: "Searching for Service"
Group students together to search for examples in the Bible of the following:

1. *Ways in which Christ served others*
2. *Stories about how people showed servanthood to others*
3. *Lessons on service/servanthood*

Divide them into groups of four or five and a few sheets of paper. Take one sheet of paper and fold it in half *(either vertically or horizontally)* to create a foldable. They will use one half of the paper to summarize the examples they find, and on the other half, they will list the scripture passages. Allow them to work in their groups for 9-10 minutes.

Guiding questions for small group Bible exploration:

1. *What kinds of things did Jesus do to serve others?*
2. *Where is it found in the Bible?*
3. *Why do you think Jesus took time to perform these acts of kindness?*

Teacher Tip: By giving your students the chance to search the Scriptures in this manner, they are becoming familiar with using keywords and phrases, concordance, and the internet to begin studying the Bible. Having them discuss a specific topic in small groups is a way to model small group Bible study. If you have other Biblical resources that can support them, then you are most welcome to make them available.

After group time ends, select a person from each group to share ONE thing that they listed in their foldable and include where it is found in the Bible. To reduce redundancy, after the first person shares, each spokesperson MUST share something different. By doing this, your students will remain engaged.

Teacher Tip: *If time permits and you REALLY want to make it interesting, have each spokesperson repeat the act that was previously shared!*

Online Teacher Tip: This activity can be replicated in an online setting by creating break-out rooms *(using the same number of students)*. Set a timer that will keep you on schedule.

Inform your students that one person will be chosen to be their group's spokesperson. So they should all be prepared to share.

Time to Teach: Before the lesson, create your own foldable that includes Christ's acts of servanthood *(a teacher copy is in the Resource section)*. Be sure to include when He washed His disciples' feet. True acts of servanthood must come from the heart.

In each example, two factors exist:

- *Jesus did not seek to become popular for what He did. He simply saw the need and addressed it. He even preached about it! Read Matthew 6: 1-4.*
- *Jesus did not expect anything back from those whom He served. Read Matthew 20: 28 and Philippians 2:4*

When we seek to be like Christ, then it will be important to follow His examples in the Bible. In Philippians 2:5-7, Paul writes that Jesus KNEW that His identity was equal to God. He was God's SON! However, He chose to give up His divine privileges so people would not feel as though they had to have a certain status before they could come to Him. Jesus became as *humble and as lowly as a slave* to invite more people to come into God's Kingdom. So as His followers, we cannot have an "I'm better than you" attitude. This does NOT demonstrate Christ's character. Reflect on the "Flip Flops" video from the beginning of the lesson and refer to the John 13 scripture where Jesus washed His disciples' feet. *Can your students see the connection between this scripture and the two factors that are part of Christlike servanthood?*

Connect It: "Full Circle Service"

Working within their previous small groups, let your students review their foldable and talk about the following questions:

1. *What kind of people did Jesus serve? Who were they?*
2. *What need was met?*
3. *What are real-life examples of serving others?*

Using their personal technology, references and/or experiences, the students will work within their group to search for people or organizations that are serving others.

Create another foldable by using another sheet of paper and folding it to create three sections instead of two.

Include the following information in a separate section:

1. *The person/organization*   2. *The act of service/need being met*   3. *A connecting scripture*

For example:

City Food Bank	*Collects food that is distributed to those who are in need (elderly, poor, displaced, disaster relief)*	Matthew 25: 34-40

The people or organizations that your students may include do not have to be well-known, popular people. Encourage them to find at least 4 or 5 examples *(one per group member)*. Once finished, give them the opportunity to share at least two from their group, especially the scripture that connects with the act of service.

Online Teacher Tip: This can be done in a remote setting using breakout rooms. Set a timer while students are in the virtual small groups. They can create their own foldables using paper that they have at their current location, OR encourage them to use their phones to make notes on what they gather about the acts of service examples they find. After this time ends you can encourage them to add their two examples to the chat box while you compile them using a Google or PowerPoint slide.

Reflect On It: "My Turn to Serve"/Service Ticket

This will be a time to have your students reflect on how they will serve like Jesus did. Serving in the Kingdom of God comes from a humble heart, then it follows with an individual passion or interest for a cause. Give students the chance to watch the following short video:

Sanya Pirani interviewed by WCCO Rachel Slavik 3/18/17

Time to Teach: This video showcases the work of a young teenager, Sayna Pirani, who had a heart for helping others. She started organizing ways to help others in need when she was eight years old! Share some details from Sanya's story *(interview transcript is in the Resource section).* Use the video to jumpstart your students' thinking on ways they can serve others who have a need. As you discuss the video, let them know that serving others does not always result in something HUGE that a lot of people know about. Serving others should be acts of love that are done to impact the Kingdom of God. Bragging and posting on social media for <u>personal recognition</u> is NOT the same thing as having a servant's heart. Remember what Jesus taught in Matthew 6:1-4 about the hypocrites who serve or pray loudly just to get attention...*we don't want to be like them!* If you are considering taking on service projects as a group, make sure to get parents' permission.

Discuss how serving others just as Christ did can become part of their lives.

1. *What are they passionate about?*
2. *Is there some concern that tugs on their heart?*
3. *What would they need to serve someone in need?*

Give each student a Service Ticket to complete as they reflect. Set up a table with the *My Turn to Serve* cards spread out. The purpose of these cards is to provide suggestions on ways that they can serve. They are organized into the following categories: *1. People to serve and 2. Ways to serve.* Let your students sort through the cards as they pray and think about how they can humbly serve others who are in need of support. *Also consider how this can become a class/group ministry service project.* Your students are not tied to select anything from the cards, as these are only meant to spark ideas. Encourage them to pray, listen and watch for what God may show them. *Recall that Sanya Pirani was only eight years old when she started her first effort to help young children!*

Serving Others

Lesson Resource Section

- ❖ *Teacher Reflection page*
- ❖ *Searching for Service Foldable Sample (for teacher)*
- ❖ *Sanya Pirani's Story (transcript from website)*
- ❖ *Service Ticket*
- ❖ *My Turn to Serve cards*
- ❖ *Object Lesson on Servanthood YouTube Link:*
  https://youtu.be/zOU2G2mdtik
- ❖ *Sanya Pirani Interview YouTube link:*
  https://youtu.be/eV6ZIrBNTAc

Serving Others: *Teacher Planning and Reflections*

<u>Before the Lesson:</u>

Journal how the Holy Spirit is leading you on this topic: **humility and serving others.** How does your attitude display Christ's characteristics? Consider *your personal spiritual journey* with this topic.

_____

_____

_____

What lesson adjustments are anticipated as you prepare for your students?

_____

_____

_____

What physical preparations need to be made for your space or extra resources that need to be acquired prior to your lesson?

_____

_____

_____

<u>After the Lesson:</u>

What questions or issues arose during the lesson that you need to cover with prayer?

List students and/or concerns:

_____

_____

_____

Searching for Service Foldable *(fold down the center)*
(for teacher reference, not an exhaustive list)

Act/Instructions on Service	Scripture Reference
Jesus washed His disciples' feet before He was to be crucified	*John 13: 1-17*
Young boy gives his food to Jesus so that it could be used to feed over 5000 people	*John 6:1-15 (The young boy had a small amount, but Jesus made GREAT use of what he had)*
Embracing being a servant	*Matthew 20:26 and 28; Mark 10:45*
Being kind to the poor	*Proverbs 19:17*
Tabitha/Dorcas' good deeds	*Acts 9:36-40*
Using gifts to serve	*1 Peter 4:10*
Serve with love	*Luke 6:35*
Reward for helping others	*Isaiah 58:10 *recommended versions: Amplified and New Living Translation*

THE STORY OF HOW IT STARTED

From a very young age, I used to worry about kids who do not have a mother and father. I used to wonder who feeds them. Who gives them clothes, especially in winter? Who keeps them warm and who reads them stories at night?

One night, I peeked in my mother's office, she was watching a YouTube video clip of children suffering due to war; I saw a girl who looked younger than me sitting on the ground with torn clothes, no shoes, immense sadness and fear in her eyes. I was sad, angry and worried for her. I ran away to my room. Her sad eyes told me "Help me."

Later, my mother had asked me what was bothering me. I told her that I saw that girl who was sitting on the ground on the YouTube video. Was it real? "Why did she look so sad and helpless?" My mother reluctantly explained that the girl perhaps lost her family and might not have anyone to care for her. I immediately asked, "Why? Mother, didn't you tell me God loves everyone?"

My Mother replied, "Of course."

"So why are some people extremely poor and others are not?" I asked.

My Mother replied, "God created people like you and others who are passionate about helping God's children."

That night my mother's words became real to me. I decided I needed to do something big to help others. Now the question in my mind was what should I do that will not only have a big impact but also to inspire my friends to collaborate with me.

The next morning I woke up early and started googling the ways to help. I came across a website that explained how I could feed a village of 100 people for one year.

Boy I was thrilled! I couldn't wait to tell my mother. When I told my plans to her she said, "How about starting with feeding one child first?"

I looked at my mother and said you told me, "I could reach for the star in me." Mother knew at this point that nothing could stop me.

Taken from: *Sanya's Hope for Children* website https://www.sanyashopeforchildren.org/

Servanthood Service Ticket

Name: _____

I have a desire to serve

_____

I can use my resources and skills to minister to them by

_____

Don't look out only for your own interest, but take an interest in others, too. You must have the same attitude that Christ Jesus had.

Philippians 2: 4-5

Servanthood Service Ticket

Name: _____

I have a desire to serve

_____

I can use my resources and skills to minister to them by

_____

Don't look out only for your own interest, but take an interest in others, too. You must have the same attitude that Christ Jesus had.

Philippians 2: 4-5

Servanthood Service Ticket

Name: _____

I have a desire to serve

_____

I can use my resources and skills to minister to them by

_____

Don't look out only for your own interest, but take an interest in others, too. You must have the same attitude that Christ Jesus had.

Philippians 2: 4-5

Servanthood Service Ticket

Name: _____

I have a desire to serve

_____

I can use my resources and skills to minister to them by

_____

Don't look out only for your own interest, but take an interest in others, too. You must have the same attitude that Christ Jesus had.

Philippians 2: 4-5

Teacher Tip: Feel free to make as many copies that are needed to accommodate your class size. Your students can make their own by using an index card or a sheet of paper (pre-cut it in half to make it stretch.

Online Teacher Tip: If you are comfortable using Google Forms, create a Google Form that includes the same ticket questions.

My Turn to Serve

Who to Serve:

These cards have people who may find themselves in need.

People who are displaced (homeless)	Young children
People with special needs	Veterans
Senior Citizens	People who are bullied
Abandoned or injured pets	People in your community
People who are disabled	People who don't have enough food in their homes
Classmates who may struggle to learn	Places in the community that need care

Ways to Serve:

These cards include suggestions on different ways to serve.

Collect canned goods	*Create Blessing Bags*	*Make cards with special messages*
Write notes or letters	*Do arts and crafts*	*Volunteer*
Participate in fundraisers	*Make friends with new people*	*Have friendly and frequent conversations*
Sing songs and read scriptures	*Play games*	*Prepare meals*
Participate in the appropriate church ministry	*Organize an event*	*Read stories*
Help in areas of need	*Work with food drives*	*Do clothes or supply drives*

Teacher Tip: Make several copies of the *My Turn to Serve* pages so students will not have to wait to review the cards. Also print each set on a different colored page to distinguish between the categories.

The Case for Obedience

Purpose: *Understand the importance of obedience.*

Learner Outcome: Make choices about obedience to God and others.

Key Scriptures: Philippians 2: 6-11; John 10 10; Genesis 22: 1-12; 1 Samuel 15; Exodus 20:12

Key Words: obey, obedience, humble

Materials: Bible, Obedience Case flags *(in Resource section)*; rope; male volunteer; parents of students OR digital photos *(gather prior to the lesson without students' knowledge)*; arts and crafts supplies

---

Set It Up: "Simon Says"

Allow students to play a round of "Simon Says" for about five minutes *(make sure students know the rules of this classic playground favorite)*.

Online Teacher Tip: "Simon Says" can be played in your online setting as well. Make sure students have their computer cameras on so that you can interact with everyone during the game.

Explore It: "Simon Says Explained"

After the game have conversations with your students about the following questions:

1. *What is "Simon Says" about? What's the "rule" of the game?*

   Participants are waiting to receive instructions from "Simon". Acting or movement without being told to do so by "Simon" results in a 'penalty'.

2. *Some people say that "life is a game". If this is the case, then what quality or behavior could this game teach you about life?*

   Obedience (following directions)

Continue with comparing this game to life by discussing these questions:

a. *So if you are a Christian, who would "Simon" be? (God)*
b. *What does "Simon" do throughout this game? (Give instructions)*
c. *What are you supposed to do when Simon says something? (Follow the instructions; be obedient)*
d. *What happens when a command is given without "Simon" telling you to do it? (Get off track; lose place in the game).*

Transition Statement: *"In order to have a relationship with God, we must understand that being obedient is expected. Today, we are going to learn how others in the Bible demonstrated obedience and why we must do the same."*

Teach It: "The Case for Obedience"
Divide students into three groups and assign them one of the following passages:

- *1 Samuel 15:17-24*
- *Genesis 22:1-12*
- *John 10:10*
- *Philippians 2:6-11*

After the groups are assigned their passages, let them know that they will be discussing the following questions:

- *Who is the main person in your Scripture passages?*
- *What was he told to do?*
- *What DID he do?*
- *What case would you make for him: OBEDIENT or DISOBEDIENT*

Give your group a set of *Obedience Case Flags* and ask them to be ready to determine which flag the person from their assigned scripture would receive *(either obedient or disobedient)*. If a group is unsure, encourage them to communicate that as well. After each flag is shared, have a group spokesperson to explain their answer.

Online Teacher Tip: For this activity you may choose to do small groups using your online conferencing platform's breakout room tools or you may choose to maintain a whole group virtual setting. Both options work well.

1. *If you choose to do virtual breakout rooms, then assign each group a passage from above and have students discuss the four questions to determine if the response to God demonstrated obedience or disobedience.*
2. *If you choose to maintain a virtual whole group, then discuss each passage with your students and allow them to determine the case. Consider the ways that students can voice their choice (virtual reaction tools, chat box response, hand or body signals such as stand up if Obedience and vice versa or make their own Obedience/Disobedience flags).*

Time to Teach: Discuss each scripture with your students and talk to them about each person's actions, and be prepared to provide background on the passages:

- For the passages about *Jesus,* explain the connection between His words in John 10:10 and His acts of obedience. For Jesus to declare, *"But I have come so that you might have life and have life more abundantly",* He had to know what He was sent to do. In Philippians 2, Paul writes that Jesus was obedient when He: *1) gave up His divine privilege; 2) took the humble position of a slave; 3) lived as a human being AWAY from God's glory in Heaven and 4) died a criminal's death on the cross.* None of these things were easy to do, but Jesus was still obedient. So just imagine if Jesus had been disobedient and what it would mean for our eternal lives!
- Your students may not initially understand that King Saul was disobedient. So be prepared to review what God commanded him to do in v 3-*to kill ALL and EVERYTHING.* After King Saul came back from the Amalekites, Samuel discovered that he had not followed God's full instructions because he brought the king of the Amalekites and the best animals that were going to be sacrificed to God. Saul thought he had done what God commanded, but he had only done part of it. In God's eyes, *partial obedience is still disobedience.*
- In the case of Abraham, he did exactly as God had instructed immediately and without hesitation. In this test of Abraham's faith, his obedience to God showed that he trusted God enough to move ahead with the task he'd been given *(to sacrifice his son, Isaac).*

Connect It: "Obedience At the Front Door"

Teacher Note: Students will have an "encounter" with their parents, either through technology or in person. *However, it will be a SECRET until it happens!* A few days prior to the lesson, speak with your students' parents or guardians and give them a brief summary of what will be discussed. Ask them if they can plan to join the class on the day of your lesson because their presence will make the lesson on obedience far more relevant.

1. *For parents who cannot be physically present, ask them for a picture and use it to create a slide presentation (at least they can be digitally present). Consider asking these parents to either write a note or record a message to their child about the importance of obedience.*
2. *For parents who are able to attend, they will not be required to speak or act in any way, just walk in and be present during the conversation. However, there will be an opportunity for them to communicate and pray with their child.*

Take a few minutes to review what has been discussed thus far in the lesson. Remind students that if the ultimate goal is to obey God, then *missing the mark* is the very definition of SIN!

Obedience is critical in their daily walk and relationship to God. *But what about in our earthly relationships and situations?* Does being obedient only apply to God? Give students examples and let them discuss, mainly in regards to parents and teachers. Once comments and responses have been made, welcome the parents into the learning space.

Time to Teach: Remind your students what obedience to God reflects: Trust and Love. Read Exodus 20:12. *What does this verse mean?* Simply put, God expects us to obey our parents or guardians. Jesus obeyed HIS Father. Obedience was part of His character. If we say that we love God but will not obey and honor the very people that He has placed in our lives to protect, guide and nurture us, then what does this reveal about our relationship with God?

Reflect On It: "A Picture of Obedience"
Give time for the parents and their children to talk about some of the key points from the lesson. Consider if this will be done collectively as a class or intimately with each family.

Create space for each family unit to create a banner or poster for their home that will be a reminder that obedience is a character of Christ that they will embrace in their homes *(1. to God and 2. to parents and others in authority)*.

If it is possible to have a blank space that can be used as a photo backdrop or a "selfie frame", then before the end of the lesson, let everyone snap a fun family picture! Encourage them to create hashtags and consider posting your photos to your church's or youth group's social media (make sure to get permission from your parents).

Teacher Tip: What's a "selfie frame"?

*Generally made from cardboard or foam, the **frame** is supposed to be used as a faux **picture frame** for a **selfie** photo, finished with either branding or some sort of commemorative slogans or text, depending on the event.*

Taken from https://www.expocart.com/blog/product-guides/our-guide-to-selfie-frames/

*If you are considering using a selfie frame, make sure to have it created in advance, and look for fun and inexpensive ideas on Pinterest!

Online Teacher Tip: This activity can be re-created at home with parental involvement. Encourage your remote participants to be creative and use items that may be meaningful for them from home. They can take a selfie and share it with others just as mentioned with the group sessions.

The Case for Obedience

Lesson Resources Section

❖ *Teacher Planning/Reflection Page*
❖ *Obedience Flags*

The Case for Obedience: Teacher Planning and Reflections

Before the Lesson:

Journal how the Holy Spirit is leading you on this topic: **Obedience**. Consider *your personal spiritual journey* with this topic.

_____

_____

_____

What lesson adjustments are anticipated as you prepare for your students?

_____

_____

_____

What physical preparations need to be made for your space or extra resources that need to be acquired prior to your lesson?

_____

_____

_____

After the Lesson:

What questions or issues arose during the lesson that you need to cover with prayer?

List students and/or concerns:

_____

_____

_____

OBEDIENCE	DISOBEDIENCE
OBEDIENCE	DISOBEDIENCE
OBEDIENCE	DISOBEDIENCE
OBEDIENCE	DISOBEDIENCE

Full Circle Ministry presents

The Character of Christ Series

For Ages 15-18

Let this mind be in you which was also in Christ Jesus!
Philippians 2:5

Online Teacher Tip Resources

Embedded in each lesson are **Online Teacher Tips.** These are suggested ideas on how to embed technology to teach the lessons. By incorporating these resources, as a Youth Pastor, Teacher or Volunteer, you have the chance to share the Gospel with more students AND involve parents as their children take part in learning the Word of God remotely. Before teaching any lesson, preparation is vital, and if you are planning to include the **Online Teacher Tips**, then make sure you are comfortable with the tools, their features and how they will be used during each lesson.

Included in the *Character of Christ* series, you will find the following online applications and/or websites, their URLs and a short description of how it may be used *(description has been taken from each tools' website):*

Flipgrid	https://flipgrid.com/	**Flipgrid** is a tool that allows teachers and students to facilitate video discussions. Each grid is like a message board where teachers can pose questions, called "topics," and their students can post their recorded responses that appear in a tiled grid display. To use Flipgrid simply create an account *(it's FREE and all students will need is their cell phone).*
Kahoot!	https://kahoot.com/	**Kahoot**! is a game-based learning platform that makes it easy to create, share and play learning games or do quizzes in minutes. Unleash the fun in classrooms and living rooms! Students can play on either their phones or on their computer. They will need to have the correct Kahoot code to enter the quiz. *And it's FREE!*
JamBoard	https://jamboard.google.com/	**JamBoard** is an interactive tool that allows students to respond to a question or activity using digital tools (their keyboard) in real time. **JamBoard** is included in Google's *G Suite* tools. Use the link to get a quick tutorial on JamBoard: https://youtu.be/S9m4HCjOkcA

Padlet	https://padlet.com/	**Padlet** is a web app that lets users post "sticky" notes on a digital wall AND be available with practically any Internet-ready device. You must create a Padlet account. You can use Padlet for free, but each free account is allowed only a certain amount of Padlets with limited features.
Google Slides	*Part of Google applications*	**Google Slides** is a presentation program included as part of a free, web-based **Google Docs** office suite offered by **Google**.
PowerPoint	*Part of Microsoft Suite Tools*	Microsoft **PowerPoint** is a presentation software that enables users to create slides, which may contain text, graphics, sound, movies, hyperlinks, and other objects.

The Mind of Christ

Purpose: *Understand what it means to be like Christ.*

Learner Outcome: Distinguish between Godly and ungodly behaviors.

Key Scripture: Philippians 2: 3-9

Key Words: character, attitude, humble/humility

Materials: Character Flags *(included in the Resources section),* index cards, wiring utensils, two small containers of water with lids: one filled with dirty water and other with clean water, two sponges, two empty containers that will be used to collect the water absorbed by the sponges, and lastly, a hand mirror for each student. You could also ask students to bring a small mirror to make your life easier.

When it is time to use the water during the Set It Up segment, make sure that students aren't able to see what's inside the containers until it's time to reveal them.

**If you have not been able to gather enough mirrors, encourage them to use their cell phones in selfie mode during the Connect It segment.*

Set It Up: "In and Out"

Teacher Tip: Prior to the class, set up the two small containers of water, the two empty containers and sponges. Since students are older, create a storyline while going through the demonstration and keep them actively engaged.

Begin by having a conversation with your students about "life experiences"—*the good and not so good*! Make note of what they mention. Explain that the covered containers of water you are holding represent those things. The two sponges may represent what happens to a person when they are hit by life's experiences *(consider naming your sponges to keep your student's attention).* Fully submerge each sponge into the separate water containers. While doing so, share that what we go through can affect our *behavior, character and mind.* After the sponges have become fully saturated, squeeze each one into a separate empty container. Talk about the differences between what came out of the sponges once they were squeezed or *placed under pressure by life's experiences.* One is clean and clear while the other one is a little more dingy and stained.

Explore It: "In and Out Explored"

After the *Set It Up-In and Out* demonstration, ask students the following questions:

1. *What would lead to the differences in the reactions/behavior/attitude of people when they are placed under pressure?*
2. *What do you know about Jesus? His behavior? His attitude? What type of pressure did Christ experience while on earth?*
3. *Based on the stories and scriptures you have read, how would you describe Jesus' behavior and attitude?*

Transition: "We are going to discover what the mind of Christ must have been like! How does knowing His mind help us to know more about who He was and His character while He was on earth?

Teach It: "Mind Dissection"

Prior to the class, cut the "Character Flags". Each flag contains words that are either characteristics and non-characteristics of Christ. However, do not share this with your students. Their task is to discover this as they sort the flags into different categories. After sorting, let students determine a name for each group of flags *(Note: Let your students label group because this will give them an opportunity to discuss the differences between the terms and lead to self discovery about the mind of Christ).*

Online Teacher Tip: Using the Character Flags, create a *Google Slides* presentation that includes the words and use one of the options below for students to interact with them. Make sure your students are unmuted so they can talk with each other.

1. *One recommendation that allows virtual interaction with your presentation is JamBoard (a Google Chrome free extension). Click on the links to view YouTube tutorials for each of these tools.*
2. Create a Kahoot!. This will allow you to do a quiz-like activity for students. In this case, use the categories (Christlike and Not Christlike) as answer choices. Or use True/False answer choices and allow students to determine the status of each Character Flag (or mix it up and challenge your kids' mental agility with Christian concepts).

Teacher Note: Make sure students can dearly distinguish between Godly and ungodly character through your questions and their responses. As they talk, encourage them to add other words for either category.

Divide students into small groups (3-5 students), and have them read Philippians 2:3-9. As they read the scripture, they should identify any significant words or phrases that describe anything about Jesus Christ based on:

1. *His status or identity (as the Son of God)*
2. *any description of circumstances He faced (even those not recorded in this passage)*
3. *His attitude and behaviors in spite of the circumstances*

From the New Living Translation, significant words are:

The same as Christ
Though He was God, He did not demand…
He made Himself nothing…
Humble position of a slave
Appeared in human form
Obediently humbled
A criminal's death

After time ends, allow them to share what they found.

Online Teacher Tip: Depending upon the conferencing platform that you use, create virtual small groups. Still allow them to have the same conversation while they are in their virtual groups. Create group roles that that everyone can be involved in the dialogue *(such as time keeper, reader, speaker, writer)*. Let your students know that they will be responsible for sharing their list with the whole group once the breakout time ends. Plan for 5-7 minutes for this virtual small group time.

Time to Teach: Have a discussion about these significant words from the scripture with students. Stress how the words they may have listed speak to Christ's identity as The Messiah. Even though Christ was The Messiah, He never boasted, became disobedient, arrogant or mean-spirited towards people He encountered. However, many of the people He met did not greet Him with open arms. His character always reflected who He said He was, which was the Son of God! What could have happened if Jesus acted in ways that were different from who He said He was. Think about the ungodly Character flags. Put into perspective how our own character and behavior affect our ability to be effective disciples. Re-read the Foundation Scripture (Philippians 2:5), and pose these questions (or feel free to add others):

- *Why is having the mind of Christ important in our daily walk?*
- *Why is our character something that we must develop?*

Revisit the sponge and the significance of squeezing it. What is in us, even though it may be buried away in our hearts and minds, is bound to come out. As followers of Christ, we have to decide if we will fully demonstrate the same mind and behaviors of Christ, in spite of what we may be experiencing.

Refer back to the following *Exploration* question: *What do you know about Jesus? What do you know about His behavior and attitude? What type of pressure did He experience while on Earth?*

If we say that we are Christians and want to live for Christ, then what will happen when life's experiences put pressure on us and we are squeezed or pushed to our limit? What is going to come out of us? What will people see? Will it affect our discipleship? Will our character glorify God? Could we say that our lives and minds are like Christ? These are all essential questions that we must consider.

Connect It: "Mind in the Mirror":

Give each student a small mirror (or ask them to use their cell phone cameras in selfie mode, but with no filters), an index card, and a pen or pencil. Give them time to quietly reflect on their character while looking at their image. Ask them to write a brief description of themselves *(their thoughts and behaviors). Is their character in church or around their family the same once they leave church and are in their community? What happens to their character when they are placed under pressure or become stressed?* Encourage them to be HONEST during this personal time. Then pair them with another student in a random manner *(example: line them up and match them from outer to inner).* During this partner discussion, instruct them to do the following:

1. Each person will have 1 minute to share his/her image reflection with their partner.
2. Then the other partner will pose the following question: *Which part of your character makes God smile?* (God smiles when our character, behavior, thoughts resemble those that Jesus displayed on earth)
3. The sharing student will respond using the following sentence stem: "God smiles when He hears or sees me…It resembles Jesus because…"
4. Once both partners have responded, they can high five and return back to their original seat.

Online Teacher Tip: Students who are remote can use their cell phones in selfie mode to complete the same task. Give them time to write their Mirror reflection before placing them in virtual breakout rooms. Follow the same instructions that are above, and encourage the peers to be honest, open and transparent as they respond to the prompts.

Reflect On It: "Reflection Smile"

Since each person has had the chance to share what part of their character makes God smile, they must address what part of their character does not look very much like Christ and needs to improve. Using the same mirror that they used for the "Connect It" activity, give them space and time to reflect on the character trait that needs to be more Christ-like. Also give them the option to record their personal message on their cell phones.

Teacher Tip: Prepare yourself to hear reasons why they can't be more like Christ. This may take one-on-one prayer with certain students. Encourage all of your students to select ONE thing, not multiple, to address in their character. God will guide them as they seek to be more holy in their walk with Him.

Closing Prayer Points:

1. *Help me to identify the parts of my character that are not Christ-like.*
2. *Show me how to display Christ-like behavior with what I say, think and do each day.*

The Mind of Christ

Lesson Resource Section

- ❖ *Teacher Reflection page*
- ❖ *Character Flags*

The Mind of Christ: *Teacher Planning and Reflections*

<u>Before the Lesson:</u>

Journal how the Holy Spirit is leading you on this topic: ***possessing the mind of Christ***. How does your attitude display Christ's characteristics? Consider *your personal spiritual journey* with this topic.

_____

_____

_____

What lesson adjustments are anticipated as you prepare for your students?

_____

_____

_____

What physical preparations need to be made for your space or extra resources that need to be acquired prior to your lesson?

_____

_____

_____

<u>After the Lesson:</u>

What questions or issues arose during the lesson that you need to cover with prayer?

List students and/or concerns:

_____

_____

_____

Character Flags

Gossip	**Meek**
Generous	**Arrogant**
Patient	**Unforgiving**
Prideful	**Humble**

Servant Leader	**Disrespectful**
Honest	**Loving**
Spiteful	**Complainer**
Self Control	**Faith**

Learning about Humility: *Footwashing Ceremony*

Purpose: *Understand what it means to act like Christ.*

Learner Outcome: Identify and model humble acts of Jesus Christ.

Key Scripture: John 13: 1-17

Key Words: humility, serve

Materials: towels, water, containers that would allow a person's foot to be submerged *(as many as needed),* liquid soap, lotion *(optional),* laptop, writing utensils, half-sheets of paper, worship music

Teacher Note: This lesson may require more time to set up. If possible, seek other available adult volunteers who would not mind supporting your youth in this experience. Keep the following things in mind: 1) space, 2) water/sink availability, 3) gender count *(it is highly encouraged to allow your female students to wash each other's feet and for males to do the same. Adult volunteers can assist with this.)*

Set It Up: "Footwashing for the Homeless"
Search for the following video clip on YouTube: **Washing Homeless People's Feet** and / or **Washing the Feel of the Homeless**.

Online Teacher Tip: Based on the online conferencing platform you use, share your screen so that students can see and hear the video. Also, consider sharing the link or YouTube video title with them so they can watch it on their phones.

Explore It: "Footwashing Video Explored"
After students have watched the video, ask the following questions:

1. *What appeared to be the primary message that was displayed in the video you watched?*
2. *In what ways is washing someone's feet being like Jesus Christ?*
3. *How was humility and service to others being demonstrated?*

Time to Teach: Highlight some of the statements that were made during the video(s). Serving others the way that Jesus served is not about notoriety and fame. It is about loving others the way God loves us, selflessly. We may never get the recognition and attention that other people get, but gaining these things should never be our goal if we are humbly serving others just as Christ did.

Teach It: "A Humility Deep Dive"
Discuss John 13 with your students using the *New Living Translation* version.

Time to Teach: Of course, we know that feet can get dirty and smell bad! The very act of touching other people's feet may seem beneath us. So for Jesus to take the time to wash His very own disciples' feet exemplified humility, especially in knowing who He is. It also showed His love for others. One way that He showed love was through serving others, although He was the Son of God *(review Philippians 2:5-8)*. Jesus did not hold back from serving the very person who would betray Him (Judas). Having the character of Christ must be something that we are committed to in our hearts, minds and bodies DAILY. During this Time to Teach, emphasize John 13:15. As the lesson continues, reinforce that Christ has given us an example of how to show love and serve others. As His followers, we are expected to do the same. Ask your students to consider what servanthood looks like in their lives.

Transition Statement: "Now that we have discussed a particular act of service that Jesus demonstrated towards His disciples, we are going to partake in a Footwashing Ceremony to understand more about what it means to emulate Christ by serving others."

Teacher Note: Make sure to monitor the pace of your lesson. Since you want the majority of your time to be spent with students participating in the Footwashing Ceremony, consider incorporating additional teaching or scriptural points during the time that students are engaged in footwashing.

Connect It: "Footwashing Ceremony and Celebration"
Explain to your students that they will partake in a foot washing ceremony just like Jesus and His disciples did. Create *female-female* and *male-male* partners in a quiet and peaceful setting. You can have your worship music softly playing in the background. Give each student a towel and explain that they will wash each other's feet.

Teacher Note: Again, the goal is not to have a long dialogue prior to this portion of the lesson, but be open to answer any questions your students may have. Help them to feel comfortable and encourage them not to joke and take this experience lightly. Use soft worship music or have other videos to show other examples of humility. Read scriptures and continue to invite the presence of the Lord into this event.

If you have students who do not wish to partake in the ceremony, pray with them in a separate setting and invite them to read the scripture again. Then ask them to make a list of other ways they could show humility and service to others who would not be able to pay them back. They should be prepared to share their list once the ceremony ends.

Online Teacher Tip: To emulate the Footwashing Ceremony for those who are participating online, this may be a great opportunity for family involvement! In this case, your students will need to gather and use their own resources. Send your parents and guardians a copy of the lesson and share the learning outcomes in advance. Support them in creating a peaceful worship atmosphere by playing music through your platform. Afterwards, give those who have participated remotely an opportunity to discuss their experiences with being able to wash another family member's feet. This experience can create valuable dialogue about the value of youth submitting to parents just as they should submit to God. Discuss how servanthood and humility can become a part of their family Christian values that are demonstrated regularly *(both inside and outside of the home)*.

Reflect On It: "Put It In A Letter"
After the ceremony has ended, give students time to reflect and consider how acts of humility can be done in their lives. Direct them to use the sentence starters to write a letter:

1. *By doing something that Jesus Christ did, I feel/understand/recognize...*
2. *I can begin to appreciate serving like Christ more by...*
3. *I will focus on ... to ensure my character is more like Christ.*

To increase your students' engagement, let them choose who they are writing to:

1. *To God, the Father*
2. *To themselves, currently or in the future*
3. *To a loved one or a spiritual mentor*

Then support them by finding a scripture that will connect them with the elements below:

- *awareness of Christ*
- *serving like Christ*
- *addressing something in their lifestyle to be more like Christ*

Closing Prayer Points:

1. *Pray for humility.*
2. *Pray for growth in servanthood towards others.*
3. *Pray to display more of Christ's character.*

Learning About Humility

Lesson Resource Section

- ❖ *Teacher Reflection page*
- ❖ *John 13 (New Living Translation)*
- ❖ *Homeless Footwashing YouTube link:*
  https://youtu.be/PIBLs5oR18w
- ❖ *Washing Homeless People's Feet*
  https://youtu.be/w_ufQLrHZZc

Learning About Humility: *Teacher Planning and Reflections*

<u>Before the Lesson:</u>

Journal how the Holy Spirit is leading you on this topic: **humility and serving others.** How does your attitude display Christ's characteristics? Consider *your personal spiritual journey* with this topic.

_____

_____

_____

What lesson adjustments are anticipated as you prepare for your students?

_____

_____

_____

What physical preparations need to be made for your space or extra resources that need to be acquired prior to your lesson?

_____

_____

_____

<u>After the Lesson:</u>

What questions or issues arose during the lesson that you need to cover with prayer?

List students and/or concerns:

_____

_____

_____

John 13:1-17 *(New Living Translation)*

Jesus Washes His Disciples' Feet

1 Before the Passover celebration, Jesus knew that his hour had come to leave this world and return to his Father. He had loved his disciples during his ministry on earth, and now he loved them to the very end.

2 It was time for supper, and the devil had already prompted Judas, son of Simon Iscariot, to betray Jesus. **3** Jesus knew that the Father had given him authority over everything and that he had come from God and would return to God. **4** So he got up from the table, took off his robe, wrapped a towel around his waist, **5** and poured water into a basin. Then he began to wash the disciples' feet, drying them with the towel he had around him.

6 When Jesus came to Simon Peter, Peter said to him, "Lord, are you going to wash my feet?"

7 Jesus replied, "You don't understand now what I am doing, but someday you will."

8 "No," Peter protested, "you will never ever wash my feet!" Jesus replied, "Unless I wash you, you won't belong to me."

9 Simon Peter exclaimed, "Then wash my hands and head as well, Lord, not just my feet!"

10 Jesus replied, "A person who has bathed all over does not need to wash, except for the feet, to be entirely clean. And you disciples are clean, but not all of you." **11** For Jesus knew who would betray him. That is what he meant when he said, "Not all of you are clean."

12 After washing their feet, he put on his robe again and sat down and asked, "Do you understand what I was doing? **13** You call me 'Teacher' and 'Lord,' and you are right, because that's what I am. **14** And since I, your Lord and Teacher, have washed your feet, you ought to wash each other's feet. **15** I have given you an example to follow. Do as I have done to you. **16** I tell you the truth, slaves are not greater than their master. Nor is the messenger more important than the one who sends the message. **17** Now that you know these things, God will bless you for doing them.

The Obedience Factor

Purpose: *Understand the importance of obedience.*

Learner Outcome: Identify the outcomes of obedience and disobedience to God.

Key Scriptures: Philippians 2:5-9; Hebrews 5:8-9; 1 John 4:20

Key Words: obedience, disobedience

Materials: 2 blindfolds, chart paper (at least 3-4 sheets), markers, blank paper, Obedience handout and Scenario cards *(included in the Resources section)*, strong male volunteer, index cards

Set It Up: "Lead Me, Guide Me"

Teacher Note: Before students arrive, create a safe "obstacle course" in your learning space. Include chairs and other objects to serve as obstructions. Because you will be giving directions to guide students through this course, make sure you have written out the directions to get from the start to the end of your specific route. To increase the course's complexity, include background noise while giving directions to the students. Although the noise does not need to be blaring, it should be loud enough to be heard and possibly distract them while they are trying to listen for your directions. Also secretly prompt one of your volunteers not to fully follow the directions that will be given in the course. So when directions are given, this student will either move in the opposite direction or not move at all.

Pre-select two students to blindfold and navigate through an obstacle course *(ask your volunteers if they will be okay to be temporarily blindfolded)*. Students will be given the task of making it through the obstacle course following the directions of the "master teacher" *(you)*.

Instruct them to listen intently to your directions as you guide them to the desired destination. Designate one additional student to be a helper to come alongside any volunteer who may get too far off the path *(this person should be calm)*. Continue this until one (or both) students finally reaches the end of the course. Be prepared to stop the students if the activity hits the 5 minute mark.

Online Teacher Tip: If possible, pre-record the "Lead Me, Guide Me" adventure using family members and/or student volunteers. Consider safely creating an obstacle course at your home (backyard) or anywhere there is enough space. Students can view the recording on the conference platform as you share your screen. If you opt to use this, then the same Explore It conversations and questions can apply.

Explore It: "Lead Me, Guide Me Explored"
After the *Lead Me, Guide Me* obstacle course, ask students the following questions:

1. *What made reaching the master teacher's destination difficult?*
2. *What helped you along the path to make it to the master teacher? In a spiritual sense, who would be the master teacher?*

Teacher Note: At this point, help students recognize that the "master teacher" is supposed to represent God and His Word. Highlight that along our walk with God we may get off track.

However, if we continue to seek to follow His Word, He is faithful enough to send "designated helpers" to support us through our journey. Ultimately obedience is what we should strive for, no matter how distractions may entice us NOT to follow.

Transition Statement: "To have a solid relationship with God, we must understand that obeying His Word is expected. Today, we are going to learn how important obeying God was to Jesus Christ and why it should be just as important to us."

Explain It: "Thoughts on Obedience"
Start by asking students to openly express their thoughts, definitions or experiences on obedience. Capture their comments using chart paper so that they can be referenced throughout the lesson. You should expect your students to have plenty of opinions about the word! After this discussion, ask them the following questions:

1. *Why do you think it is so difficult to be obedient?*
2. *Do you think that obedience has a place in our relationship with God?*
3. *Why do you think obedience to God is important?*

Online Teacher Tip: Consider one of the following two options to engage your students in this discussion:

1. *Create a **Flipgrid** and allow students to use their Smartphones to record their responses to the questions above (make sure they have the code to access your Flipgrid. Once this is complete, everyone will be able to see each other's short video.*
2. *Invite your students to share their comments using any online Chat Tools that may be available on the conferencing platform being used.*

Time to Teach: Remind students of the student volunteer who did not follow the instructions of the "master teacher" during the *Set It Up* activity. That person repeatedly got "off track". In real life, when we habitually find ourselves getting off track and missing, there are consequences that follow....sooner or later! And *missing the mark* is the definition of <u>sin</u>. God's love for us covers all facets of our lives. Obeying God 1) *demonstrates our love to Him; 2) keeps us from getting off track or sinning* which 3) *covers us from paths of self-destruction or unholy living.*

Divide students into groups of four and distribute the "How Important Is Obedience to God in My Daily Walk" handout. Students should first read Philippians 2:5-9 and Hebrews 5:9. Afterwards they will answer the following questions *(Questions are included in the Resource section)*.

1. *Who do both of these scriptures refer to? (Jesus)*
2. *In both of these scriptures, what is being discussed about Jesus? (His obedience)*
3. *What happened as a result of Jesus's obedience? (God blessed His name to be great)*
4. *Therefore, what can be concluded about the result of obedience to God?*

Online Teacher Tip: Create breakout rooms using your online platform *(no more than four students)*. To ensure that all students get a chance to participate in the virtual small group, have them number themselves based on how many are in the groups. Whichever number they are assigned will be the question that they will lead for discussion in their group.

Time to Teach: Obedience to God has always been expected and did not start only when Jesus was physically on the earth. Recall the story of Abraham, Isaac and the ram in the bush. Abraham is chronicled in the Bible because of his immediate response to doing what God told him to do *(sacrifice his only son, Isaac)*. Obeying God does yield results. However, these results are not always tangible (revisit point 3 from the previous *Time to Teach)*. Although Jesus Christ was the Son of God, He was still expected to obey His Heavenly Father (Hebrews 5:8). Even though His obedience led to a cruel death on the cross (Philippians 2:8) Jesus still did what God told Him to do. In both of these situations (with Abraham and Jesus), the following things were demonstrated:

- Obeying God can be a test of our faith.
  - *God, I trust that You will keep me through whatever You assign me to do because I know it will increase my faith*
- Obeying God shows that we love Him
  - *Lord, I'm going to do just what You've told me to do.*

Obeying God is essential to our Christian character because we are doing what Christ did.

After reading and discussing the Obedience handout, ask students to reconsider the following question that was posed earlier:

Do you think that obedience has a place in our relationship with God?

Time to Teach: Discuss how obedience (or lack thereof) affects their daily walk with God. Share these Biblical truths:

- *The greatest commandment is to love God by keeping (obeying) His commandments.*
- *John 14:15 reads, "if you love me, you will obey what I command."*
- *When we are being obedient to God, we are doing just that: knowing Him, loving Him and having an intimate relationship with Him.*
- *We must be attentive to God's laws. This is not an option, because we cannot have an intimate relationship with Jesus and disregard what He taught.*

If you are open or feel led by the Holy Spirit to give a personal example, feel free to open up and discuss this with your students.

Teacher Note: Whether you are presenting this lesson face-to-face or remotely, your students' parents will be invited to make an appearance AFTER you have the discussion with your students based on the italicized questions below. Try to keep this discussion to no longer than 5 minutes.

Online Teacher Tip: It is a good idea to have a "moderator" or someone to support you with the online platform tools. Either pre-direct your parent to log on at a specific time, and if you have a platform that has a waiting room *(such as Zoom)*, as parents log on, then you (or your moderator) can give them access at the designated time in your lesson.

After the *Explain It* discussions, ask students to reflect upon their previous remarks about obedience and the *Set It Up* activity. The risk of not paying attention was missing the target, and the *Ultimate Target* is God. As they learned today, the Obedience Factor is critical in having a solid spiritual relationship. *So how important should obedience be when it comes to other relationships and situations? Or does obedience only apply to God?* Allow your students to freely discuss these questions. If parents are present, open the door and allow the "special guests" to enter the room. If parents were not able to be there, use whatever visual format you may have prepared that includes their pictures.

Time to Teach: Now that your guests of honor have made their entrance, ask students to provide a recap of the lesson. God gave us parents or guardians. The Bible speaks about children obeying their parents in the Lord because it is right. Since this was a commandment from God *(Exodus 21:12),* then obeying parents lines up with obeying God! So what about obeying other individuals in authority, such as teachers, school administrators, law enforcement or bosses? Will we always want to follow every rule or expectation that is in place? Probably not! Ask your students to give examples of rules they may not want to follow (from anyone or any setting) or to share any experience in which they chose NOT to be obedient. It is easy for us to see the connection of obeying the Spiritual laws and commands and God. However, we must understand that what was written in 1 Samuel 15:22 can be applied to our daily lives as well. Laws and rules are set for a purpose. Forsaking their purpose because we may not like or understand them or the person/people/organization that made them can lead to personal and unnecessary sacrifices. As we seek to know more about God's instructions for our lives, pray that He will make our hearts more humble to abide by His words. Before closing this discussion, give parents and their teens time to dialogue about obedience to God and in all other aspects of their lives.

Connect It: *"Obedience At the Front Door Demonstration"*

Teacher Note: This demonstration will show your students what obedience and disobedience look like when trying to model the character of Christ. Ask a parent if he/she would be open to serving as a volunteer for the demonstration *(should be strong enough to withstand being pulled by a rope).*

Securely and tightly tie a rope around your volunteer's waist. This person will represent "God's Words". Students will take turns reading an Obedience Scenario. After each scenario is read, ask them to determine if this is a case of *obedience* or *disobedience*. Your volunteer will move based on the following:

- *Whenever <u>obedience</u> is demonstrated, the parent volunteer and student reading the card will begin to walk side-by-side and engage in a shoulder embrace.*
- *Whenever <u>disobedience</u> is demonstrated, the volunteer will stand with feet planted firmly as your student attempts to pull away in the opposite direction with the rope.*
  - Whenever disobedience occurs, we are going against God. His Word is unchanging. Moving away from God in disobedience would result in going against the covering, protection and provision.
  - *This means the same thing when disobedience to parents occurs. However, unlike with parents who, at times, can be talked into changing their minds and "giving in", God's commands are constant and unchanging (read 1 Samuel 15:29 Amplified preferred).*

Online Teacher Tip: Select one of the short videos to show to your students and discuss afterwards:

<u>Act of Obedience</u>   <u>A Short Obedience Video</u>

Reflect On It: "Obedience Renewal"

To close this lesson, consider the following options:

1. For those parents who are able to come and participate in this lesson, allow them and their children to have this time together. Give them time to discuss this topic of obedience and how this lesson can remind them of what it should look like at home. If any parent/child group seeks counsel on this matter, use the Bible and/or Pastoral Support as the foundation.
2. Give students the chance to create a **Six-Word Memoir** *(use the link to share examples)*.
3. The topic of the memoir will be ***Obedience***.

Online Teacher Tip:

There are several resources that can be incorporated into this *Reflect On It* segment:

- If your students will be creating a six-word memoir, invite them to share it in the chat feature. *Encourage students to unmute their microphones and encourage them to share their memoir.*
- *Create a* Padlet *and instruct your students to add their responses to the wall. If you select the Padlet option, you can download the QR code and students will be able to access the Padlet directly from their smartphones. Prior to sharing the QR code or link, make sure the privacy settings are set to: "visitors can write".*

To put a fun spin on it, extend it as a "homework" assignment so they can write a rap or song based on their memoir. Encourage them to record and share it with their classmates for the next lesson.

*When you create a free Padlet account, then your submissions will be saved.

Closing Prayer Points:

1. *Pray for a heart of obedience for God's Word.*
2. *Pray for a heart of obedience towards parents, teachers, coaches and others in authority.*
3. *Pray to respond with a good attitude when expected to be obedient.*

The Obedience Factor

Lesson Resource Section

- ❖ *Teacher Reflection page*
- ❖ *Obedience to God in My Daily Walk Handout*
- ❖ *Thoughts on Obedience Discussion Questions*
- ❖ *Obedience Scenario Cards*
- ❖ *Six-Word Memoir Description*
- ❖ *Act of Obedience YouTube link:*
  https://www.youtube.com/watch?v=lq_dYdceY9Y&feature=youtu.be
- ❖ *A Short Obedience Video YouTube link:*
  https://youtu.be/vdU1tAblO60

The Obedience Factor: *Teacher Planning and Reflections*

<u>Before the Lesson:</u>

Journal how the Holy Spirit is leading you on this topic: **Obedience**. Consider *your personal spiritual journey* with this topic.

_____

_____

_____

What lesson adjustments are anticipated as you prepare for your students?

_____

_____

_____

What physical preparations need to be made for your space or extra resources that need to be acquired prior to your lesson?

_____

_____

_____

<u>After the Lesson:</u>

What questions or issues arose during the lesson that you need to cover with prayer?

List students and/or concerns:

_____

_____

_____

How Important is OBEDIENCE to God in my Daily Walk?

Obedience to God is very important in your Christian growth. No one in this life will ever become sufficiently sanctified to the point where they are always obeying the law, but we can honor and maintain obedience to God by meditating on the words and actions of Jesus Christ.

The greatest commandment is to love God by keeping *(obeying)* His commandments.

Matthew 28: 36-38 reads, *"Teacher, which is the greatest commandment in the Law?" Jesus replied, 'Love the Lord your God with all your heart and with all your soul and with all your mind' This is the greatest commandment."*

You ask, "How important is obedience to God?" In the gospel of John, obedience to God is [communicated] time and time again. John 14:15 reads, *"if you love me, you will obey what I command."*

The great commandments are reiterated in Matthew 22:36-40, which reads, *"Teacher, which is the greatest commandment in the Law?" Jesus replied, "Love the Lord your God with all your heart and with all your soul and with all your mind. This is the first and greatest commandment. And the second is like it: "Love your neighbor as yourself". All the Law and the Prophets and on these two commandments."*

Jesus is very concerned about us, and he wants us to do more than just participate in good works, He wants us to believe in him. He wants us to come up higher and be "like" him. When we are being obedient to God, we are doing just that, *knowing Him, loving Him, and having a personal, intimate relationship with Him*. To do this, we must be attentive to God's laws. This is not an option because you can't have an intimate relationship with Jesus and trample on the words He taught. Being obedient to God is not the same as sticking to the speed limit because you get a fine if you disobey. Obedience to God is living God's Word because you want to enjoy being filled with the love of Jesus.

We must believe in Jesus, we must have faith and trust in Him. Calling ourselves a Christian on its own won't do. Just following the commandments won't do either. Reading the Bible diligently won't do. **We have to take the Word into our hearts**. When we make the transition from calling ourselves a "good Christian" to being someone who is having a **deep personal and intimate relationship with the Lord**, then we can receive the fullest measure of God's love and power each and everyday of our lives.

That is the essence of <u>obedience</u> to God

*Adapted from blog found on the website AllAboutFollowingJesus.org

Thoughts on Obedience Group Discussion Questions

1. *What person do both of these scriptures refer to?*	2. *In both of these scriptures, what is being discussed about Jesus?*
3. *In both of these scriptures that discussed Jesus, what happened as a result of Christs' obedience?*	4. *Therefore, what can be concluded as a result of obeying God?*

Obedience Scenario 1

Juan's Scenario

Juan really wants to go to his friend's house down the street, so he asked his dad if he could go. His dad said that he would take Juan AFTER he finished everything that he was supposed to do at the house *(homework, housework).*

But Juan is ready to go NOW because his friend has been talking about the new game he just got. So he decides to walk to his friend's house. He didn't tell his dad that he left the house.

What verdict does Juan receive:

Obedience or Disobedience

Obedience Scenario 2

<u>Chris's Scenario</u>

At home, Chris is a good boy and does what his dad tells him to do at home. But when he gets to school, that's another issue!

There's always an argument that occurs when Chris is given directions or reminded to follow a rule. He even talks back to his basketball coach! He admits that he doesn't like his coach, and his teachers are NOT his parents. So they "can't tell him nothing" because they don't have the authority to talk to him about following team or school rules!

What verdict does Chris receive:

Obedience or Disobedience

Obedience Scenario 3

Jason's Scenario

Jason goes to Sunday School every week and hears his teacher teach that God expects His children to love their enemies. So Jason knows what he should do.

But when Jason goes to school, he is constantly being bullied by another student. Even though his friends tell him to physically fight back or to get revenge, Jason decides to pray for this classmate. Sometimes it's not easy to do, so Jason prays that God will protect his heart from lashing back out at this person.

What verdict does Jason receive:

Obedience or Disobedience

Obedience Scenario 4

Peter and Andrew Scenario

When Jesus was walking by a lake, he saw two brothers, Peter and Andrew, who were busy doing their jobs *(fishing)*. Jesus told the brothers to stop what they were doing and come follow him. The two brothers immediately left what they were doing and began to follow Jesus.

So Peter and Andrew became Jesus' first two disciples.

Matthew 4: 18-20

What verdict do Peter and Andrew receive:

Obedience or Disobedience

Obedience Scenario 5

Tiana's Scenario

Tiana wants to visit her friend who lives on another street. She asked her mom for permission to go, but her mom said, "No, not today because I need some help around the house."

Tiana really wants to go to her friend's house, but she also recognizes that her mom has told her that she can't go today. So she asks her mom what needs to be done and starts to help her mom.

What verdict does Tiana receive:

Obedience or Disobedience

Obedience Scenario 6

Troy's Scenario

Troy's father told him to get up and mow the lawn. But Troy replied that he was busy playing a game on his phone. So he didn't initially follow his father's instructions.

Troy's father had to tell him six more times before Troy finally got up to mow the lawn.

What verdict does Troy receive:

Obedience or Disobedience

Obedience Scenario 7

Noah's Scenario

God told Noah that He was going to destroy the earth because the people had become very evil. He told Noah to build an Ark and gave him very specific instructions on how to build the boat and what to do once it was built.

Even though Noah had never seen an Ark before, he followed all of the instructions that God gave him and built the Ark exactly as it had been described by God.

Genesis 6:9-22 (emphasis on v 22)

What verdict does Noah receive:

Obedience or Disobedience

Obedience Scenario 8

<u>Jesus Scenario</u>

Jesus was the Son of God. God told Him that He would have to die a painful death on the Cross in order to save humankind from going to hell.

People talked about Jesus and although He had the power to destroy them all, He chose not to.

When they hung Him on the Cross, Jesus could have gotten down, but instead, He chose to stay there and do what His Father had told Him to do.

Matthew 26:36-44

What verdict does Jesus receive:

Obedience or Disobedience

What is a Six-Word Memoir?

A six-word memoir is just that; *six words that have been selected to define, summarize or articulate the meaning of a particular topic.*

The words that are used do not have to rhyme, but they must make sense and relate to the topic.

Six-word memoirs are meant to be personal expressions of one's feelings towards or experiences with the subject matter.

Some examples of six-word memoirs that relate to Christ are below:

- *Died for you. Keep in touch.*
- *Sent to save. Condemned. Will return.*
- *Behold, I make all things new.*
- *Loved you unto death, on cross.*
- *Started our carpenter. Significant career change.*
- *Radical service, radical love. Follow me.*
- *Humble to death on a cross.*

After sharing these examples with your students, allow them to write their own Six-Word Memoir on <u>Obedience</u>.

Printed in the USA
CPSIA information can be obtained
at www.ICGtesting.com
LVHW061221060924
789972LV00011B/289